T0152580

BRENDAN J. BARNICLE

FINANCIAL ANXIETY

A little book on faith & money

Morehouse Publishing
NEW YORK

Copyright © 2021 Brendan J. Barnicle

All rights reserved. No part of this book may be reproduced, stored in a retrieval system, or transmitted in any form or by any means, electronic or mechanical, including photocopying, recording, or otherwise, without the written permission of the publisher.

Unless otherwise noted, the Scripture quotations contained herein are from the New Revised Standard Version Bible, copyright © 1989 by the Division of Christian Education of the National Council of Churches of Christ in the United States of America. Used by permission. All rights reserved worldwide.

Church Publishing Incorporated
19 East 34th Street
New York, NY 10016

Cover design by Jennifer Kopec, 2Pug Design
Typeset by Progressive Publishing Services

Library of Congress Cataloging-in-Publication Data
A record of this book is available from the Library of Congress.

ISBN-13: 978-1-64065-462-4 (paperback)
ISBN-13: 978-1-64065-463-1 (ebook)

Contents

Introduction:
Everyone Worries about Money . . .

Almost everyone worries about money. I worry about money, and most of the people that I know worry about money. However, very few people, particularly in church, talk about their financial anxiety. In many ways, money remains a taboo topic. While the church has led conversations about other taboo topics, like sexuality, death, and illness, money remains elusive. One rector told me that he knew more about people's colons than about what was in their wallet.

It may come as no surprise then that money is also our biggest source of stress. In a 2015 survey, the American Psychological Association (APA) found that 72 percent of Americans reported feeling stressed about money at some time in the prior month. At the time, APA CEO Norman Anderson noted that "Regardless of the economic climate, money and finances have remained the top stressor since our survey began in 2007."[1] Furthermore, the APA found that stress related to financial issues is having an

---

1. "American Psychological Association Survey Shows Money Stress Weighing on Americans' Health Nationwide," American Psychological Association, February 4, 2015. https://www.apa.org/news/press/releases/2015/02/money-stress. Accessed September 28, 2020.

increasingly negative impact on Americans' health and well-being. More recently, in 2019, in an annual survey by financial services firm John Hancock, 68 percent of respondents reported experiencing financial stress, and 71 percent reported worrying about having financial difficulties. The survey also found that stress is affecting worker productivity. In the survey, 49 percent of respondents reported that their financial stress was making them less productive at work.[2] Financial stress has continued to mount as people have contended with the COVID-19 pandemic and its economic impacts. As a result, a lot has been written about financial stress. Understandably, most of the writing has focused on sound financial practices and mental health advice. As the conversation has developed, however, the importance of faith has not been sufficiently recognized in the conversation.

This Little Book addresses how the Christian faith may help us to cope with financial anxiety and how it might help us to care for each other when experiencing financial anxiety. Addressing financial anxiety is more than just a pastoral care issue, it is also a justice issue. Generally, people with the fewest resources experience the greatest financial anxiety, but not exclusively. Wealthy people experience financial anxiety, too. The current global economic system fuels financial anxiety; in fact, it requires financial anxiety

---

2. "John Hancock 2019 Financial Stress Survey, 1, 2, 5." https://assets. jhnavigator.com/managed_assets/itemFiles/USA/Financial_Stress _Whitepaper_Secured_FINAL_10.28.19.pdf. Accessed September 28, 2020.

to propel its growth. From mounting consumer debt to targeted internet advertising, the global economy encourages people to buy more things, which drives up their financial anxiety for a variety of reasons. Some experience anxiety because of the things that they think that they should have, but do not have, and others experience anxiety because of the debt that they have as a result of their purchases. Finally, some find themselves living in poverty, where financial anxiety is a constant part of life. In 2019, 10.5 percent of the U.S. population lived below the national poverty level, according to the U.S. Census Bureau.[3] According to the World Bank, global poverty was expected to rise in 2020 for the first time in a generation. As many as 703 to 729 million people are projected to be living on less than $2 per day.[4] Dismantling financial anxiety may start with pastoral care, but it can only end with a more just and equitable economy. The Baptismal Covenant calls on us to strive for justice and peace among all people. Financial anxiety is the result of injustice and disrupts God's peace. Therefore, it requires our action.

This book primarily focuses on pastoral care, which is a critical first step toward justice, but this is not meant to diminish the central importance of justice when discussing money. This Little

---

3. Jessica Semega, Melissa Kollar, Emily A. Shrider, and John Creamer, "Income and Poverty in the United States: 2019," U.S. Census Bureau, Report Number P60-270, September 15, 2020. https://www.census.gov/library /publications/2020/demo/p60-270.html. Accessed November 17, 2020.

4. The World Bank, "Poverty: Overview," October 7, 2020. https:// www.worldbank.org/en/topic/poverty/overview.

Book examines what Christianity can tell us about financial anxiety. Chapter 1 discusses the causes of financial anxiety, focusing on materialism, idolatry, mimetic desire (that is, the desire to have what others have), envy and rivalry, and individualism. Chapter 2 analyzes what Christian theology and scriptural interpretations can tell us about financial anxiety. Can we really follow Jesus's directive in Luke 12:22, " . . . do not worry about your life, what you will eat, or about your body, what you will wear"? Chapter 3 examines how scripture might help identify our financial anxiety. What does it mean if I understand money in terms of the widow's two copper coins (Mark 12:41–44 NRSV) or the rich young man (Mark 10:17–31 NRSV)? Chapter 4 offers pastoral responses to financial anxiety. What can we really do to ease our own financial anxiety and then help each other cope with financial anxiety? This Little Book certainly cannot answer all the concerns about financial anxiety. It can, however, start a conversation: a conversation that is long overdue. As God's people, we are called to lives of faith, hope, and love, and to the extent that financial anxiety limits our lives, it limits God's grace, and it requires our urgent attention. Let's start that conversation.

1 ▪ What Are We Afraid Of? Financial Anxiety Inside and Outside of Church

Generally, people are anxious about money because they fear that they do not have enough of it. Without enough money, they fear for their safety and well-being. A recent study from PNC Advisors found that even wealthy people do not feel that they have enough money. To envision feeling secure, most people believe that they need twice as much money as they currently have, regardless of their net worth.[5] The research surveys conducted for this book confirmed these findings. In fact, in some of the surveys, people with the lowest incomes reported less financial anxiety than those with mid-level incomes. Generally, however, financial anxiety is inversely related to income. The higher your income, the less likely that you will experience financial anxiety. Sometimes, wealthy people are embarrassed by their wealth or the ways in which they earned it, and they are equally uncomfortable talking about their financial anxiety. It seems that no one can escape financial anxiety. Yet, ironically, no one wants to talk about it, which only feeds the anxiety.

In the surveys and focus groups completed for this book, respondents had both financial anxiety and a strong Christian

---

5. Jim Wallis, *Rediscovering Values: A Guide for Economic and Moral Recovery* (New York, NY: Howard Books, 2011), 110.

faith. Yet, relatively few had any interest in hearing about money in church. When people think about conversations around money in church, many automatically assume that the church will be asking for money, and they tune out the topic altogether. Other people find money and church completely irreconcilable. They come to church to elevate their soul, and money does the exact opposite for them. Survey respondents claimed little interest in classes on theology and money or discussions of money during worship. Yet, they were open to innovative ways of talking about money in church. For example, there was a lot of interest in applying the Trinity to personal finances. If we refer to the Trinity as Creator, Redeemer, and Sustainer rather than Father, Son, and Holy Spirit, what might it mean to spend our money in ways that are creative, redemptive, and sustaining? If the Trinity is a community of three persons, what would it mean to spend our money in ways that are cooperative, communal, and anti-competitive, like the Trinity? Could a Trinitarian approach to money reduce our financial anxiety? Or, would it merely shift the focus? Could it help create a more just economy? These questions intrigued people in the focus groups for this book, and they are the types of questions that can drive a theological discussion of financial anxiety.

For now, let's consider the theological reasons for financial anxiety. The church is exactly the right place to start a theological discussion of financial anxiety and money. There are several very practical reasons for financial anxiety. The global economy is changing rapidly, and people are increasingly uncertain about their financial futures. It is estimated that 47 percent of the current workforce have positions that could be replaced by robots, and 55 percent of current workers do not have sufficient resources to retire.[6] Furthermore, ongoing changes in existing work create disruption, uncertainty, and depletion, all of which further augment financial anxiety. Unbridled anxiety has numerous negative outcomes. It limits the human capacity to learn, magnifies differences, encourages scapegoating, and fosters division; all of which are readily apparent in our surroundings.[7] Various social and economic policies can help to offset some of these dramatic economic changes, and theology and scripture can also help addresses these uncertainties.

Aside from the practical challenges of financial anxiety, there are some spiritual challenges that make financial anxiety even more difficult. Theologically, financial anxiety has roots in materialism, idolatry, mimetic desire (that is, the desire to have what others have), envy and rivalry, and individualism. These themes run throughout scripture and Christian theology. Considering the ways in which the church has discussed these topics might help us to understand how to cope with our own financial anxiety and how to care for others who experience it.

Materialism

Since the 1960s, social scientists have observed an increase in materialism, "a preoccupation with or stress upon material rather than

---

6. Peter L. Steinke, *Uproar: Calm Leadership in Anxious Times* (Lanham, MD: Rowman & Littlefield, 2019), 15.

7. Steinke, *Uproar,* 18.

intellectual or spiritual things,"[8] around the world. There are several factors driving growing global materialism, but perhaps the biggest factor is the need of individuals for identity and a sense of self. Material objects help us to define ourselves, and advertisers have only reinforced the power of their brands to do that. Products have become aspirational. At some level, advertisers have convinced us that their products will make us happier and healthier. Therefore, in challenging times, people are increasingly turning to material things to define themselves. In their 1981 book, *The Meaning of Things: Domestic Symbols and the Self*, sociologists Mihaly Csikzent-mihalyi and Eugene Rochberg-Halton concluded that "things embody goals, make skills manifest and shape the identities of their users."[9] Material possessions are not inherently wrong. In fact, material objects can enhance individual and congregational experiences of spirituality and God.[10] However, when people become too dependent on material things to define their lives, then the material can become a problem. Ultimately, material items fail to satisfy human desires, and they lead to only greater anxiety and the desire for more things. As a result, materialism can drive envy and rivalry. Cszikzentmihalyi and Rochberg-Halton advised striking a balance between material objects and one's self-perception. Since their work

8. Merriam-Webster Dictionary, https://www.merriam-webster.com /dictionary/materialism.
9. Mihaly Csikzentmihalyi and Eugene Rochberg-Halton, *The Meaning of Things: Domestic Symbols and the Self* (Cambridge, UK: Cambridge University Press, 1981), 1.
10. de Leeuw, *The Body of Christ*, 3.

was published in the early 1980s, people have not heeded their advice. As the social scientists have discovered, we have not become less materialistic since the 1980s, but only more materialistic, and not just in some countries, but across the globe.

Well before Cszikzentmihalyi and Rochberg-Halton, Jesus and many Christian theologians warned about the risk from materialism, and they argued for simple lifestyles that were not dependent on material things. The Patristic Fathers, Thomas Aquinas, twentieth-century Msgr. John Ryan, S.J. and most recently, bestselling author Brené Brown have all argued, in various ways, for a "virtue of sufficiency."[11] A "virtue of sufficiency" suggests that people keep only the money that they need to support themselves, and they share the rest with others. This virtue presupposes that God's abundance is sufficient to take care of everyone as long as people are willing to share with each other. However, the virtue of sufficiency runs into a challenge when it comes to the specifics of what is sufficient. What is sufficient for one person might not be sufficient for another. Today, some are continuing to work toward the establishment of guidelines for sufficiency. One recent example is the Plenitude Movement. The Plenitude Movement encourages people to embrace a world of abundance rather than scarcity. The Plenitude Movement is founded on four principles: moderation in hours worked; making things for oneself; an

---

11. Brené Brown, *The Gifts of Imperfection: Let Go of Who You Think You're Supposed to Be and Embrace Who You Are* (Center City, MN: Hazelden Publishing, 2010), 83.

environmentally aware approach to consumption; and investment in other people and in our communities.[12] These communities share their resources and barter their goods and service. The Plenitude Movement is new, but similar movements are not new. They follow in a long tradition of intentional communities that valued simplicity. From the Rule of St. Benedict to St. Francis of Assisi's embrace of poverty, from Amos Bronson Alcott's transcendentalist commune to the Catholic Worker communities, many have tried to offer alternative economic lifestyles and a new understanding of sufficiency. Individuals have consistently been open to looking at ways of living outside of materialism. Yet, despite these valiant efforts, materialism continues to gain strength around the world.

Materialism has two direct impacts on financial anxiety. First, it creates anxiety because people do not believe that they have enough things. They believe that they need more things to fully define themselves. This anxiety can manifest as hoarding at one extreme and excessive frugality at the other extreme. We all want to be acknowledged and appreciated by others, and sometimes, we may come to believe that possessions will help us win that attention. Excessive materialism has become an acceptable community norm. Many people want to have more than their peers. In fact, studies show that people care more about their relative

---

12. Juliet B. Schor, *Plentitude: The New Economics of True Wealth.* (New York: Penguin Press, 2010), 4–7.

economic position than their absolute position.[13] As a result, billionaires continue to pursue more wealth, even when they have no conceivable way of spending it all. Finally, we can be deathly afraid of downward mobility.[14] Downward mobility is an anathema to the American Dream, and some will go to tremendous lengths to limit that prospect. Therefore, materialism puts people in conflict with each other, in efforts to outdo each other and limit their losses. Rather than reinforce materialism as a community norm, Christians could start to develop alternative norms. We will talk more about those possibilities later in the book.

Materialism also creates financial anxiety when we buy things that we cannot afford. Financial anxiety can manifest as overspending. As a result, people rack up enormous consumer debt, which creates ongoing anxiety in the struggle to pay those debts off. Debt has the potential to reduce people to a number and to reduce people, who are equal in God's eyes, into a dominant creditor and a subordinate debtor. The Israelites understood the disorienting impact of debt and sought to manage it with prohibitions against usury, the Jubilee's cancelation of debts, and the Sabbath.[15] Psalm 37:21 even suggests that it is virtuous to forgive debts and a blessing to have one's debt forgiven. "The wicked borrow, and do not pay back, but the righteous are generous and keep giving"

---

13. Robert Skidelsky and Edward Skidelsky, *How Much is Enough: Money and the Good Life* (New York: Other Press, 2012), 149.
14. de Leeuw, *The Body of Christ*, 78–79.
15. de Leeuw, 12–14.

(Ps. 37:21 NRSV). The Israelites also realized that money was meant to flow through the economy. When one individual accumulated a lot of wealth, then there was less money to flow through the economy. Conversely, the more the money flowed through the Israeli economy, the more the people benefited from it. Therefore, the Israelites rightly feared that accumulated wealth and debt would disrupt the economy's proper functioning.

The causes of financial anxiety are addressed in much of the current secular writing on the topic. There are several practical personal financial solutions, like creating budgets, following one's credit score, and working with a financial advisor. These are all sound practical steps, but they do not address the underlying causes of materialism and financial anxiety: idolatry, mimetic desire, envy and rivalry, and individualism. Fortunately, a theological discussion of financial anxiety can start to address all of these issues.

Idolatry

For Israel, there was a strong focus on the second commandment prohibiting idolatry. "You shall not make for yourself an idol, whether in the form of anything that is in heaven above, or that is on the earth beneath, or that is in the water under the earth. You shall not bow down to them or worship them . . ." (Exod. 20:4–5 NRSV). The Israelites also had their own experience with idolatry when they created the Golden Calf (Exod. 32:4 NRSV). They understood how attractive it was to have a physical idol that can stand in for an invisible God. There are many things that can become idols in our lives, but money is one of the most common. Money can easily serve as a stand-in for God. It can fund armies and industries, and it can have enormous impact on politics and culture. In a world that cannot see God, money can be a very tangible idol. As people become more and more obsessed with the things that others have, they can make idols of those things or of the money that it takes to get those things or of the people who already have them. In the twenty-first century, there are a number of idols other than money: possessions, celebrity, power, sex, and financial security. The internet platforms also increase the chance of idolatry. They increase our focus on products and on other people's lives, which makes idolatry seem ordinary, rather than dangerous. Even financial security, ironically, can become an idol. In pursuit of financial security, people can justify the relentless pursuit of wealth.

The writers of Deuteronomy understood the link between idolatry and desire. " . . . Do not covet the silver or the gold that is on them and take it for yourself, because you could be ensnared by it; For it is abhorrent to the LORD your God" (Deut. 7:25 NRSV). Biblical scholar Walter Brueggemann points out that this language and the language that follows in Deuteronomy 7:26 reveals a deep concern that coveting things is dangerous because those things that we covet frequently become idols for us, and draw us away from God and from each other.[16] Idolatry undermines our commitments to God and to each other, and much idolatry springs from desire.

---

16. Brueggemann, 39.

Mimetic Desire

Once we make something into an idol, then we start to desire it more intensely. Conversely, once we desire something intensely, we can start to make it into an idol. In 1961, philosopher René Girard introduced the theory of the "mimetic nature of desire" in his first book, *Deceit, Desire and the Novel.*[17] His theory posits that people desire the things that they see that others have. In an increasingly connected and global context, mimetic desire can extend to virtually everyone and everything. Furthermore, our economic system seeks to reinforce need and desire as a way to drive ongoing sales. If people did not already feel that they needed what others have, advertising has encouraged their desire and validated it. Subsequently, people feel even greater pressure to have the things that other people have in their lives. More colloquially, this might also be called "the fear of missing out." No one wants to miss out on the fun or pleasure that others might be experiencing in their lives.

Internet platforms only make us more aware of what we are missing. In fact, internet platforms have accelerated mimetic desire. These platforms understand our desires better than we understand them ourselves. Moreover, the algorithms that run these platforms know how to manipulate our desires. In a manner, these platforms are manipulating the free will that God has provided to us, just

---

17. Rene Girard, *Deceit, Desire and the Novel.* Translated by Yvonne Frecerro (Baltimore, MD: Johns Hopkins Press, 1965), 24.

like other forms of addiction. The internet platforms are designed to manipulate us into spending more time on their platforms, so that their advertisers can sell more things to us. In addition, as we spend more time on the internet platforms, the platforms learn more about us, which enhances their ability to manipulate us and our desires. The business models behind these internet platforms are designed to turn our wants into our needs, which drives financial anxiety. In fact, in the recent documentary *The Social Dilemma*, several of the people who developed these platforms warn against the inherent dangers of these platforms. They point out that the algorithms are constantly getting better at outsmarting our brains, and our brains are not evolving quickly enough to keep up with them. As we fall further behind, these platforms and their advertising interests have an increasing ability to drive our materialism, our desire, our anxiety, and our unrest.

In biblical terms, mimetic desire is known as covetousness. For Israel, there was a strong focus on the tenth commandment. "You shall not covet your neighbor's house; you shall not covet your neighbor's wife, or male or female slave, or ox, or donkey, or anything that belongs to your neighbor" (Exod. 20:17 NRSV). The Israelites understood that desire drives coveting, and that coveting can be incredibly powerful, seductive, and disruptive. Israel had experienced it. The book of Genesis documents Pharaoh's endless coveting, and the tragedy that his coveting brought upon Israel. When the Israelites were in Egypt, they were forced to work endlessly and in poverty to help satiate the Pharaoh's unrelenting fear of not having enough grain to sustain himself and his court during a famine. In a different context, also in Genesis, the sons of Jacob abandoned their brother Joseph to slavery because they coveted their father's attention. Coveting is not only about desiring what belongs to another; it also includes seizing what belongs to another.[18] The Israelites were aware of covetousness, but the threat from covetousness is even greater today. Covetousness is rarely viewed as a sin in modern culture; it may be called ambition or enthusiasm. Yet, covetousness has dire consequences. The sin of coveting can carry over to other sins, including stealing (sixth commandment), adultery (seventh commandment), and bearing false witness (eighth commandment). In fact, biblical scholar Brueggemann argues that covetousness ultimately leads to idolatry (second commandment), rather than the other way around. Therefore, biblical scholars have suggested that the tenth commandment is really a catch-all commandment, because it is the first step toward violating other commandments.[19] Girard concluded that prohibitions, like the Ten Commandments, are attempts to control mimetic desire.[20] The people who developed these prohibitions were well aware of the destructive power of mimetic desire. Therefore, the prohibitions are designed to limit desire, envy, rivalry, and violence, which inevitably develop if mimetic desire goes unchecked.

---

18. Brueggemann, 38.
19. John Durham, *Word Biblical Commentary: Exodus* (Grand Rapids, MI: Zondervan, 1987), 298.
20. Girard, 16.

Envy and Rivalry

Envy and rivalry can quickly emerge from mimetic desire. People are constantly comparing themselves to others; we build our identities in this way. We care deeply about what others think of us. When we cannot get what we see that others have, then we become envious of others and bitter rivalry can develop between people. The Rev. Dr. Gawain de Leeuw points out that envy actually reflects a fear of loss, and it increases our dissatisfaction with the world and the anxiety in our lives.[21] If envy is unchecked, it can grow into rivalry. Rivalry can seed hate, contempt, and even violence. Throughout the Old Testament, there are stark reminders of the destruction of rivalry: Cain and Abel (Gen. 4:1–16 NRSV), Sarai and Hagar (Gen. 16 NRSV), David and Uriah (2 Sam. 11–12 NRSV), Jacob and Esau (Gen. 25:19–34 NRSV), and Ahab and Naboth (1 Kings 21:1–15 NRSV).[22] Again and again, scripture demonstrates the disastrous effects of rivalry. Rivalry tears apart the body of Christ, and destroys God's creations.

To manage rivalry, people resort to all sorts of behaviors that are contrary to the Gospels. There can be violence; there can also be theft, adultery, and bearing false witness. A more contemporary response to rivalry is shopping. To avoid feeling inferior to others, people turn to consumption. They buy the products that they believe will make them look like they are doing better than others, in hopes that others will envy them. This cycle can be isolating.

---

21. de Leeuw, *The Body of Christ*, 26–27.
22. de Leeuw, *The Body of Christ*, 26.

People find that they would rather be isolated from others than develop personal relationships, because relationships can be risky. Once we are in relationship with others, we risk envying the other person and developing new potential rivalries.[23] So, sadly, we often conclude that it is better to be alone than to manage the envy that might come from developing friendships. This perverse logic tears at the body of Christ and divides us, which is completely contrary to Jesus's continuous attempts to unite us.

Jesus demonstrated how humans can live beyond rivalry. He redirected his disciples away from rivalry toward a new notion of a good life—one that included rest and joy. He also taught practices to his disciples that would help them to alleviate rivalry: praying in private; taking the lowest seat at the table; rejecting status.[24] He encouraged his disciples to avoid public attention, so that they would not attract the envy of others, and develop rivalries. When the mother of James and John asked Jesus to put her sons at his right and left in his kingdom, Jesus politely asked if they are willing to suffer as he will suffer (Matt. 20:20–28 NRSV). When Jesus overhears the disciples bickering over who was the greatest among them, Jesus says "All who exalt themselves will be humbled, and all who humble themselves will be exalted" (Matt. 23:12 NRSV). In the same situation in Luke's gospel, Jesus says that "the least among all of you is the greatest" (Luke 9:48 NRSV).

---

23. de Leeuw, *The Body of Christ*, 136.
24. de Leeuw, *The Body of Christ*, 129.

Jesus is the anti-rival, and he provides a model for individuals, congregations, and denominations of how to move beyond envy and rivalry. Rather than modeling our behavior and our desires on other people that we see in the world, Jesus provides a different model and alternative community norms. Jesus's ministry demonstrates anti-competitive ways to live that transcend mimetic desire, envy, and rivalry. He models this practice when he graciously accepts the anointing of his feet by a woman, most like Mary Magdalene, who comes to visit him (Matt. 26:7; Mark 14:3–7; Luke 7:36–50; John 12:1–8 NRSV). The disciples complain about the expense of the ointment, and of the background of the woman. Jesus can see the envy and rivalry emerging among the disciples. So, Jesus explains his appreciation for her love and gratitude, and he assures the disciples that she has been redeemed. Jesus's world is not one of accounting for every penny, but one that is transfixed on love. His world moves beyond the desires and envy of this world. Similarly, he moves his disciples beyond counting each sin. When he is confronted with an adulterous woman, he does not rush to judge her. Rather, he says, "Let anyone among you who is without sin be the first to throw a stone at her," and all of her accusers leave her (John 8:7 NRSV). Jesus embodies love that is not competitive, not envious, and not rivalrous. Jesus demonstrates ways of living beyond rivalry.

In addition, Jesus is also clear not to make rivalry into the new rival. He does not seek to destroy rivalry. In destroying rivalry, Jesus would destroy a part of human beings that God created. Instead, Jesus calls us to live with the desires that God has created in the world, and to turn them back toward God. The family systems theory therapist and Jewish rabbi Edwin Friedman would call Jesus, the "non-anxious presence," the person who can confront, but not exacerbate, the surrounding anxiety.[25] Jesus plays this role again and again. When confronted by the Pharisees, the Sadducees, the Herodians, the Samaritans, and even by Satan, Jesus does not become anxious. He does not worry about rivals. He turns his focus back to God and back to love. It is challenging for everyone to live out the gospel. Congregational leaders cannot ignore the human capacity for resentment and rivalry. Instead, they need to create ministries and spaces that redirect that negative energy back toward love and toward God.[26]

These rivalries are not only limited to individuals. Rivalries develop between congregations and denominations. Congregations and denominations compare themselves to each other. They experience the same underlying mimetic desire that individuals experience, and they may be even less equipped to discuss it than individuals. Any discussion of money in an Episcopal church is likely to lead to comparisons to other churches and complaints about the diocese. Rather than avoiding these topics, these conversations offer an opportunity to explore the underlying emotions. In some ways, it may be safer for people to discuss these topics in

25. Edwin H. Friedman, *A Failure of Nerve,* 10th anniversary rev. ed., ed. Margaret M. Treadwell and Edward W. Beal (New York: Church Publishing, 2017), 16.
26. De Leeuw, *The Body of Christ,* 179.

the context of a congregation or a denomination, rather than in the context of their own lives. Potentially, churches can offer guidance to individuals as they confront their desires and rivalries. Rejecting rivalry can have economic consequences that can help to free people from financial anxiety. When we stop consuming to compete with each other, we can be liberated from possessions, and start to connect with each other. As theologian Eve Poole observes, "Desire is part of the human condition, and our spiritual task is not to resist it, but to curve it away from materialism back towards God."[27] Having open conversations about desire and rivalry lays the groundwork for strong theological discussions of money, and for dismantling financial anxiety.

Individualism

Finally, individualism is also compounding financial anxiety. A 2017 study published in *Psychological Science* found that individualism is increasing around the world. According to the study, individualism has increased globally by 12 percent since 1960.[28] Individualism is also directly correlated to economic development. As an economy strengthens and grows, individualism grows along with it. There are cultural differences in the ways that individualism

---

27. Eve Poole, *Buying God: Consumerism & Theology* (New York: Church Publishing, 2019), 99.
28. "Individualistic Practices and Values Increasing Around the World," Association of Psychological Science, July 17, 2017. https://www.psychologicalscience.org/news/releases/individualistic-practices-and-values-increasing-around-the-world.html.

is expressed, but it is on the rise around the world. People are prioritizing themselves, their time, and their resources over others.[29] Internet platforms have also accelerated these trends. As a result, people are finding themselves lonelier and more vulnerable. In a culture that says that everyone is supposed to look after themselves, there is little urgency in helping others. When people are not confident that they can turn to others for help, their anxiety naturally increases, particularly their financial anxiety.

In the United States, individualism has almost become an idol unto itself. American individualism is rooted in New England Puritanism and in Jeffersonianism; it is reflected in both the Declaration of Independence and the U.S. Constitution. Individualism and personal freedom have been important to the development of the culture, politics, and economy of the United States. In the nineteenth century, romanticism and individualism became the predominant schools of thought in the United States and Europe. In fact, Rene Girard asserts that in the twentieth century, researchers and philosophers became afraid to even challenge individualism, because of the "political and social imperatives of their community."[30]

---

29. Henri C. Santos, Michael E. W. Varnum, and Igor Grossman, "Global Increases in Individualism," in *Psychological Science*, 2017;28(9):1228–1239.

30. René Girard, *Things Hidden Since the Foundation of the World*. Translated by Stephen Bann and Michael Metteer, (Stanford, CA: Stanford University Press, 1978), 7.

Despite its popularity in academic, economic, and political circles, individualism is not endorsed in scripture. In fact, the gospel attempts to move humans beyond an individualistic interpretation of scripture to a communal focus.[31] Rather than focus on individual salvation, scripture describes a "new heaven and a new earth" that includes all of God's creation (Isa. 65:17; Rev. 21:1 NRSV). The same communal focus applies to money and possessions. Paul reiterates a focus on a communal economy in 2 Corinthians 8:1–15. He commends the community in Macedonia for their support of other communities, despite their own poverty. Giving from their poverty reflected Christ's "law of neighborliness," which was present in the early Church and based on covenantal Judaism.[32] In covenantal Judaism, all possessions were believed to have come from God, and, therefore, all possessions needed to be shared among all of God's people. In fact, Judaism viewed individualism as a risk. If someone had too much autonomy, that person might lose sight of God. Warnings against self-sufficiency appear in Deuteronomy 8:17 and Psalm 10:4, 6.[33] "Do not say to yourself, 'My power and the might of my own hand have gotten me this wealth'" (Deut. 8:17 NRSV). "In the pride of their countenance the wicked say, 'God will not seek it out'; all their thoughts are, 'There is no God'" (Ps. 10:4 NRSV). "They think in their heart,

31. Brueggemann, 15.
32. Brueggemann, 237.
33. Brueggemann, 120.

'We shall not be moved; throughout all generations we shall not meet adversity'" (Ps. 10:6 NRSV).

Ironically, despite the heavy focus on individualism in the United States, individualism may not actually even exist in the modern world. People are entirely dependent on each other. In fact, there are metaphysical and epistemological views that suggest that our minds are not truly independent and that "our choices are merely perceptions in a highly determined universe."[34] The Rev. Dr. De Leeuw challenges notions of individuality, and suggests the existence of "interindividuality."

> In mimetic theory, human consciousness is therefore inter-individual. While a person may perceive being individuated, or separate from other people, their consciousness cannot be neatly disentangled from the outside influences of other people. Desires are not invented internally from a blank slate, but learned. A person's tastes and a worldview arise out of family, community and culture.[35]

Instead of actual individuality, there is an illusion of individualism, which serves the economic market forces well. If people believe that they are individuals, then they are encouraged to find those ways to express their individuality, and those expressions come largely through possessions. Cars and clothes are used to demonstrate individuality. However, a focus on individuality risks envy,

---

34. de Leeuw, *The Body of Christ*, 75.
35. De Leeuw, *The Body of Christ*, 126.

rivalry, and ultimately, a loss of care and compassion for others. It can result in egotism and a lonely life that becomes consumed with the next acquisition.

In contrast, Jesus offers a life of community, in which we are all part of the same body of Christ. While people may have different roles in the body and while they may not like other parts of the body, they are still part of a single body of Christ. The church offers opportunities for people to enter into community, and it offers it in a way that is essentially equal for all. When we gather at Eucharist, everyone receives the same thing. We each get a small bit of the bread and cup. As a result, there is little opportunity for envy and rivalry. Like Jesus, the church can be an anti-rival that enables people to move beyond perceived individuality and its resulting anxiety, and into blessed community and God's abundant love.

Money Systems

The surveys for this book demonstrated the challenge of leading a theological discussion of money and financial anxiety; money can be an emotional trigger for people and for organizations. Bowen family systems theory maintains that conflicts over money in families or congregations are never really about the money, but reflect the deeper anxiety in the system.[36] Therefore, if approached

---

36. Margaret J. Marcuson, *Money and Your Ministry* (Portland, OR: Marcuson Leadership Circle, 2014), Friedman, *A Failure of Nerve*, 67; Peter L. Steinke, *Congregational Leadership in Anxious Times* (Lanham, MD: Rowman & Littlefield, 2006), 14–15.

properly, a conversation about money can actually open up a conversation about challenges in a system. In addition, these conflicts and conversations can expose triangulation in a system. Triangles exist in every system. Triangulation occurs when people do not speak directly to each other but through a third person. The analysis of these triangles within a family or congregation can help people to see when there are anxieties in the system. Money provides a critical lens for individuals, families, congregations, and even denominations to better understand themselves, and ultimately, to provide ways of coping with financial anxiety and caring for those experiencing it. Therefore, when coupled with the proper resources, people can use conflict as an opportunity to demonstrate that it is possible to dismantle financial anxiety and strengthen the people of God.

Because money is such a sensitive topic, theological discussions of money require adaptive change, rather than technical quick fixes. Harvard professors Ronald Heifetz and Marty Linsky have described a sharp distinction between adaptive change and technical quick fixes. Adaptive change requires changes in culture and attitudes; therefore, adaptive change frequently meets resistance. As a result, many leaders will default to technical quick fixes, which are changes that utilize existing know-how and the organization's existing problem-solving approaches. Attempts to change the way that a congregation or its members view financial anxiety will likely require changes to culture and attitude. Adaptive changes often make us uncomfortable. Therefore, it is likely to meet with resistance. Some of this resistance was clearly voiced in the open responses to the surveys completed for this book. People thought that the questions about money and church were "weird," "irrelevant," or "inappropriate." Like any adaptive change, leaders will need maturity and patience. Dismantling financial anxiety might be challenging for many people. The pastoral program presented in chapter 4 provides resources to initiate theological conversations about financial anxiety. The program includes congregational forums and exercises. The exercises are pedagogical tools designed to help people discern how God is calling them to view money, possessions, and financial anxiety. Even with resources, this will not be easy work. Leaders will need to reiterate the importance of this work.[37] They will need to be willing to say that "the buck stops here," and provide the financial leadership necessary for individual, congregational, and denominational health and growth.

---

37. Ronald Heifetz and Marty Linsky, *Leadership on the Line: Staying Alive Through the Dangers of Change* (Boston, MA: Harvard Business Review Press, 2017), 55, 75, 141.

2 ▪ What Has the Church Said? Scriptural and Theological Guidance on Money

While the folks I talked with before writing this book resisted discussing money in church, the biblical scholar Walter Brueggemann argues that economics actually sits at the core of the biblical tradition.[38] There are 500 references to prayer in the Bible, and two thousand references to money and possessions.[39] Jesus frequently discussed money. In fact, he mentioned it second only to the kingdom of God. By one count, 62 percent of Jesus's parables refer to money and possessions.[40] This should not be surprising since he came from a Jewish tradition that was keenly focused on the theological and biblical aspects of money. The book of Genesis and the Psalms declare that all things, including money, come from God, and Deuteronomy insists that money needs to be

---

38. Walter Brueggemann, *Money and Possessions* (Louisville, KY: Westminster John Knox Press, 2016), xix.
39. Michael Schut, ed. *Money & Faith: The Search for Enough* (New York: Morehouse Publishing, 2008), 39.
40. Ibid, 39. Michael Packer, "Jesus Talked the Most About . . . Money?" Smyrna Patch, last modified July 24, 2011. http://patch.com/georgia /smyrna/jesus-talked-the-most-aboutmoney; Richard J. Foster, *Celebration of Discipline: The Path to Spiritual Growth*, Special Anniversary Edition (New York: HarperOne, 2018), 83.

managed with an eye on justice.[41] Jesus was familiar with Deuteronomy's prohibition on usury and the calls for Sabbath, a Year of Release and Jubilee; all of which sought to free people from institutionalized debt and economic inequality.[42] Jesus also realized the centrality of money to people's lives, both physically and spiritually. He said, "Do not store up for yourselves treasures on earth, where moth and rust consume, and where thieves break in and steal; but store up for yourselves treasures in heaven, where neither moth nor rust destroy and where thieves do not break in and steal" (Matt. 6:19–20 NRSV). Money serves as a kind of mirror that reveals who people are to the world; it provides the opportunity to demonstrate generosity and compassion or to display greed and hoarding. Therefore, money can be a source of anxiety and also, for followers of Christ, it is an opportunity for discipleship.

Judeo-Christian teachings mandate sharing our money and possessions with others. It sounds like a very simplistic solution; sharing is what we were taught in kindergarten and Sunday school. Yet, sharing remains the only way to overcome human desire and establish right relations with our money, which also makes sharing the only way to overcome financial anxiety. Sharing provides a way of maintaining a detachment from possessions, so that our possessions do not drive us away from God, but help us to develop a greater attachment to God and to God's children. Theologian

---

41. Brueggemann, *Money and Possessions*, 5.
42. Ibid, 53.

William Cavanaugh writes that the "insatiability of human desire" can only be satiated by the grace of the Eucharist.[43] In addition to Eucharist, Cavanaugh proposes a broad range of ways for us to share with others.[44] Cavanaugh's suggestions reinforce the communal nature of the work of theological discussions of money and financial anxiety. It is a communal project that is well documented in the history of the church.

A Brief Overview of Christian Theological Views of Money

The early Christian church adapted two different and somewhat conflicting views of wealth, which may explain Christians' persistent confusion regarding the proper relationship between faith and finance. On one hand, Jesus was deeply skeptical about money and possessions, but on the other hand, he recognized the importance of money for providing support and hospitality to those in need.[45] Biblical scholar Sondra Ely Wheeler characterizes these approaches to wealth as peril and obligation, each of which demands different behavior.[46] If wealth and possessions are perilous, then one should give them all away. But if wealth and possessions impose a responsibility, then those

---

43. William Cavanaugh, *Being Consumed: Economics and Christian Desire,* (Grand Rapids, MI: William B. Eerdmans, 2008), 54.
44. Cavanaugh, *Being Consumed,* 57.
45. Luke Timothy Johnson, *Sharing Possessions: What Faith Demands,* 2nd ed. (Grand Rapids, MI: William B. Eerdmans, 2011), 19.
46. Sondra Ely Wheeler, *Wealth as Peril and Obligation* (Grand Rapids, MI: William B. Eerdmans, 1995), 46.

entrusted with them are required to use their resources for the care of others.

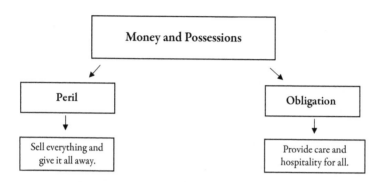

Jesus expressed both perspectives. His suspicion about money is evident in the "great reversal," when he preached that the "the last will be first, and the first will be last" (Matt. 20:16 NRSV).[47] His suspicion also appeared in his response to the "rich young ruler," who he directed to sell everything and follow him (Matt. 19:16–29, Mark 10:17–30, Luke 18:18–30 NRSV).[48] Conversely, he commends the rich tax collector Zacchaeus for paying back those whom he had defrauded and for giving half of his possessions to the poor (Luke 19:9 NRSV). Jesus understood that money could be a source of redemption and forgiveness.

47. Justo L. Gonzalez, *Faith and Wealth: A History of Early Christian Ideas on the Origin, Significance, and Use of Money* (Eugene, OR: Wipf & Stock Publishers, 2002), 76.
48. Gonzalez, *Faith and Wealth*, 76.

The Sermon on the on the Mount also captures these two views of wealth. Jesus begins by reinforcing the importance of almsgiving and the obligations of wealth. "Give to everyone who begs from you" (Matt. 5:43 NRSV). But Jesus proceeds to advise his listeners to rely upon God for material possessions: "No one can serve two masters . . . You cannot serve God and riches" (Matt. 6:35 NRSV). Since these admonitions are not entirely consistent, it is understandable that Christians have implemented them in different ways over the last two thousand years. To sort out the confusion, communities have repeatedly attempted to set standards. Community standards for wealth and possessions have appeared in the Decalogue, Deuteronomy, the Acts of the Apostles, and Benedict's Rule of Life. Yet, even after two thousand years of talking about money, many are as confused as ever about how to use it in ways that are consistent with their faith. In the surveys for this book, Christians continued to struggle when discerning how to use their money individually and congregationally. In focus groups, it was clear that people knew that they needed to share, but they were unclear about who, what, where, and how to share. There is a tremendous need for formation for individuals and congregations on what to do with their money. Formation could provide direction, which could ultimately alleviate financial anxiety. While a theological conversation on financial anxiety will not eliminate these struggles, it will help people, congregations and denominations to identify the immediate pastoral needs and long-term inequity that must be addressed to reduce financial anxiety.

In conversation with the numerous scriptural references to money and possessions, Christian theology offers an abundance of financial guidance. Theologians of most every era have discussed money. The early church embraced a preference for poverty, and shared Jesus's suspicion of wealth.[49] In the third century, the Christian writer Tertullian warned:

> If anyone is worried by his family possessions, we advise him, as do many biblical texts, to scorn worldly things. There can be no better exhortation to the abandonment of wealth than the example of our Jesus who had no material possessions.[50]

Chapters 2–5 of Acts of the Apostles illustrate how the early Christians shared their money communally, and established community standards.

> All who believed were together and had all things in common; they would sell their possessions and goods and distribute the proceeds to all, as any had need (Acts 2:44–45 NRSV).
>
> Now the whole group of those who believed were of one heart and soul, and no one claimed private ownership of any possessions, but everything they owned was held in common (Acts 4:32 NRSV).

---

49. Gonzalez, *Faith and Wealth*, 110.
50. Richard Rohr, *A Lever & A Place to Stand: The Contemplative Stance, the Active Prayer* (Mahwah, NJ: The Paulist Press, 2001), 52, citing Tertullian, *The Apology in The Ante-Nicene Fathers*, Hendrickson Publishing, 1995.

The early church continued to reflect Jesus's suspicion of wealth, but it also began reiterating the importance of using wealth to care for others. Much like their Jewish ancestors, it embraced community standards for wealth and possessions. Community discernment and community standards were crucial for adoption of financial expectations at that time, and they are equally important now. Without community standards, it is difficult to develop a shared theology of money. Without a shared theology of money, it is unlikely that individuals will change their behavior and address their financial anxiety. Generally, we respond to community norms because we want to be accepted by our community; we want the approval of the community. People particularly look to money as a way to win that approval. Therefore, when financial norms are articulated in a community, then people are likely to change their behavior. In the simplest terms, we are more likely to share when we see that others are sharing.

Jesus recognized that there was intense financial anxiety in the world, and he attempted to reduce it by insisting on hospitality.[51] If you are confident that other members of the congregation will care for you, then your financial anxiety is likely to decline. The early church understood this, and it embraced the Jewish tradition of caring for the poor, which was a sharp contrast to the prevalent pagan view at the time.[52] In addition to the Acts of the Apostles,

---

51. Gonzalez, *Faith and Wealth*, 78.
52. Peter Van Nuffelen, "Social Ethics and Moral Discourse in Late Antiquity" in *Reading Patristic Texts on Social Ethics*, ed. Johan Leemans, Brian J. Matz and Johan Verstraeten (Washington, DC: Catholic University of America Press, 2011), 54–55.

the Didache includes early references to community ownership.[53] The Didache, which means "teaching" in Koine Greek, is a first-century Christian treatise that includes three sections covering Christian ethics. It is considered the oldest extra-biblical source for information about Christianity, and it provides strong guidance for sharing. The epistle of Barnabas, which scholars believed was written around 135 CE, also describes sharing community assets.[54] Second-century Apostolic Father Hermas was concerned that wealth was an impediment to salvation.[55] Therefore, Hermas, along with Clement of Rome and Ignatius of Antioch, proposed almsgiving as a means for the wealthy to share their resources and to care for the poor.[56]

As the pre-Constantinian church attracted wealthier people, its position on wealth became more ambiguous. It spoke less about the peril of wealth and more about its obligations. It focused increasingly on the ways in which money could be used for the care of the poor and for building up the church. Sharing was still encouraged, but the focus changed on how to share and with whom. Second-century Greek Bishop Irenaeus shared his predecessors' suspicion of wealth, but he did not advocate a complete renunciation of all goods. Instead, he expected Christians to use their goods "for righteousness even while knowing that they are

---

53. Gonzalez, *Faith and Wealth*, 93.
54. Gonzalez, *Faith and Wealth*, 95.
55. Gonzalez, *Faith and Wealth*, 97.
56. Gonzalez, *Faith and Wealth*, 101.

not rightful belongings, and even knowing that they are the result of unrighteousness."[57] Second-century theologian Clement of Alexandria foreshadowed a virtue of sufficiency. He wrote, "Just as the size of the foot determines the size of the shoe, so should the needs of the body determine what one possesses."[58] As it grew, the early church moved away from the complete renunciation of wealth. Instead, it encouraged a detachment from wealth, and theologians started to develop a virtue of sufficiency. Fourth-century Greek Bishop Basil of Caesarea criticized the aggressive accumulation of wealth and proposed a sufficiency test. A sufficiency test holds that individuals keep only the money and property that they need for survival, and to share the rest of their wealth with others.[59] In listening to all of these voices, the church was attempting to discern its community standards for wealth and possessions. As a result, the church was also starting to address underlying financial anxiety. Just like today, the church had a hard time reaching consensus.

Discernment was particularly difficult because early church leaders generally came from the upper classes. Those leaders had not experienced the same financial anxiety as others had.[60] Furthermore,

---

57. Gonzalez, *Faith and Wealth,* 111.
58. Gonzalez, *Faith and Wealth,* 115.
59. Brian Matz, "The Principle of Detachment," in *Reading Patristic Texts on Social Ethics,* ed. Johan Leemans, Brian J. Matz, and Johan Verstraeten (Washington, DC: Catholic University of America Press, 2011), 183.
60. Pauline Allen, "Contemporary Catholic Social Teaching" in *Reading Patristic Texts on Social Ethics*, ed. Johan Leemans, Brian J. Matz, and Johan Verstraeten (Washington, DC: Catholic University of America Press, 2011), 35.

many of them had walked away from lives of wealth and privilege, and they chose a life of simplicity and poverty. Yet, they were reluctant to challenge the status quo. While many contemporary theologians point to the Desert Fathers' support for the preferential option for the poor, the text and the context are not quite as clear.[61] Later theologians became more explicit about supporting and encouraging wealth. In early 300 CE, Lactantius' *Divine Institutes* provided one of the first clear defenses of private property.[62] In addition, Lactantius criticized Plato and other philosophers who were suspicious of wealth.[63] These early voices became the dominant voices in the church once the church became a sanctioned institution of the Roman Empire. They established the theological standards for money and possessions, which maintained the status quo and limited the opportunity for broader community discernment about financial anxiety.

Over the centuries, many have continued to remind Christians of the perils of wealth, but they have also reinforced the need for money for hospitality. Francis of Assisi called money "dung," and he continually stressed the need to care for the poor.[64] In his own

---

61. Johan Leemans and John Verstraeten," The (Im)possible Dialogue between Patristic and Catholic Social Thought," in *Reading Patristic Texts on Social Ethics*, ed. Johan Leemans, Brian J. Matz, and Johan Verstraeten (Washington, DC: Catholic University of America Press, 2011), 223.
62. Gonzalez, *Faith and Wealth*, 137.
63. Gonzalez, *Faith and Wealth,* 139.
64. Dan Runyon, "St. Francis of Assisi: The Joy of Poverty and the Value of Dung" in *Christian History Magazine, Volume VI, No 2, 1987*. https://christianhistoryinstitute.org/magazine/article/francis-of-assisi-on-poverty-and-dung

life, he left familial wealth. He famously stripped himself naked and walked away from his family home to stress the significance of detachment from material things and money. Attempts to guide Christians in their use of money continued in the eighteenth century, in the work of the American preacher Jonathan Edwards and in the nineteenth century, in the work of the Anglican leader Frederick Denison Maurice. Edwards, who was known for harsh "fire-and-brimstone" preaching, also wrote *Christian Charity: The Duty of Charity to the Poor*.[65] He opened his book with a quote from Deuteronomy, "If there is among you in need, a member of your community in any of the towns within the land that the Lord your God is giving you, do not be hard-hearted or tight-fisted toward your needy neighbor (Deut. 15:7 NRSV)." He then proceeded to detail the obligations that Christians have to those without resources, and refuted any objections to sharing. Maurice introduced Christian Socialism, because he found capitalism was far too selfish for Christians, and he found it inconsistent with Jesus's vision of the reign of God.[66] Congregational leaders, like Edwards and Maurice, demonstrated how money could be used as a tool for God's beloved community, and they attempted to bring their congregations along with them. While they did not find universal adoption of their ideas, they re-engaged a theological discussion of money that had laid largely dormant.

---

65. Marek P. Zabriskie, ed., *The Social Justice Bible Challenge: A 40 Day Challenge* (Cincinnati, OH: Forward Movement, 2017), 12.
66. Zabriskie, 12.

Today, church leaders like Pope Francis and Archbishop of Canterbury Justin Welby are continuing to draw Christians into a theological discussion of money. In his 2013 papal encyclical *The Joy of the Gospel (Evangelii Gaudium)*, Pope Francis warned of the growing idolatry of money, and he challenged his readers to understand that "We need to say 'thou shall not' to an economy of exclusion and inequality."[67] In his first book, *Dethroning Mammon*, Archbishop Welby demonstrated the kind of financial leadership that will help the church to move forward with a theological discussion of money. As a former financial executive, Welby offered an unapologetic view of the economic markets and materialism. He concluded that the markets attempt to frighten people with the threat of scarcity. By contrast, Jesus demonstrated God's abundance and generosity. Archbishop Welby concluded that Christians need to train themselves to see God's abundance in the world, just like Jesus did.[68] For example, he suggested that we ought to see a church budget not as merely a spreadsheet, but as practical theology, demonstrating how a congregation applies its theology in the world.[69] With such strong statements from two major religious leaders, how could congregational leaders not see an obligation to lead a theological discussion of money as part of their ministries?

---

67. Kevin. E. McKenna, *A Concise Guide to Catholic Social Teaching*, 3rd ed. (Notre Dame, ID: Ave Maria Press, 2019), 67.
68. Welby, *Dethroning Mammon*, 126.
69. Welby, 126.

In the United States, financial anxiety can be particularly challenging to discuss. Wealth has not only been viewed as a peril and an obligation, but also as a blessing. There is scriptural support for this view, but it risks idolatry and injustice. It also accelerates financial anxiety, because it makes money a gift from God. Therefore, under this reasoning, if you are poor, then you also are not one of God's chosen ones.

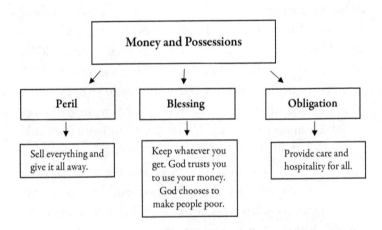

Throughout the Old Testament, there are recurring references to wealth as a form of blessing for God's faithful chosen.[70] Contemporary prosperity theology builds on these ideas, but these ideas are not actually new in the United States. They are deeply ingrained in Christian theology. Starting with English and American Puritans in the eighteenth century, wealth was viewed

---

70. Wheeler, *Wealth as Peril and Obligation*, 125.

as God's gift for the righteous, and a reward from God.[71] During the early twentieth century, several business leaders made enormous fortunes that they attributed to God. Standard Oil founder John D. Rockefeller considered himself God's "wise and responsible steward" of his wealth.[72] He believed that God intended him to spend money as only his conscience would dictate. In the 1920s, Henry Ford became an "amateur theologian" arguing that machinery was "the New Messiah."[73] Over the years, there have certainly been divergent voices that cautioned about the danger in viewing wealth as a blessing. Social gospelers, Christian Socialism, Catholic Workers and others tried to return the United States to a notion of wealth as peril and obligation, but they have found little support.[74] The view of wealth as a blessing for a lucky few removed the possibility of community discernment over standards for wealth and possessions. It also enshrined individualism, and even selfishness. The theology of money became dictated by those who controlled the money, and the other voices were removed from the conversation, which is one more explanation for the difficulty in starting theological conversations of financial anxiety in churches today.

---

71. Eugene McCarraher, *The Enchantment of Mammon: How Capitalism Became the Religion of Modernity* (Cambridge, MA: Belknap Press of Harvard University Press, 2019), 117.

72. McCarraher, *The Enchantment of Mammon*, 194.

73. McCarraher, *The Enchantment of Mammon*, 362.

74. McCarraher, *The Enchantment of Mammon*, 351, 353.

Sharing

Throughout scripture and Christian theology, sharing wealth and possessions is a recurring solution to challenges posed by money. Biblical scholar Luke Timothy Johnson proposes that all of scripture demands sharing possessions, both as a "mandate and symbol of faith."[75] In the Pentateuch, there is a deep covenantal relationship between God and God's people, and that covenant requires the sharing of possessions because all things come from God's.[76] The Prophets and the Psalms reiterate that sharing is the only reasonable response to God's creation.[77] The Letter of James provides more explicit instruction.

> If a brother or sister is naked and lacks daily food, and one of you says to them, 'Go in peace; keep warm and eat your fill,' and yet you do not supply their bodily needs, what is the good of that? So, faith by itself, if it has no works, is dead. (James 2:15–17 NRSV).

The gospels also reiterate these guidelines. Repeatedly, Jesus encouraged and mandated open-ended caring and financial support for others. In his parable of the Good Samaritan, after rescuing the Jewish victim of a crime, the Samaritan takes the man to an inn where he will be cared for, and the Good Samaritan assures the innkeeper that he will pay for all the costs of the victim's care

---

75. Luke Timothy Johnson, *Sharing Possessions: What Life Demands*, 2nd ed. (Grand Rapids, MI: William B. Eerdmans, 2011), 73.
76. Johnson, *Sharing Possessions*, 81.
77. Johnson, *Sharing Possessions*, 89.

upon his return through the region. "The next day he took out two denarii, gave them to the innkeeper, and said, 'Take care of him; and when I come back, I will repay you whatever more you spend'" (Luke 10:35 NRSV). God gives us the gifts that are necessary for living and for giving, and God mandates that we freely share those gifts. Similar to Sondra Ely Wheeler, Johnson recognizes that money and possessions are a potential danger, but they are also necessary to provide hospitality, which is an exercise of faith and love of God in giving to others.[78] Ultimately, Johnson concludes that how individuals share their God-given possessions is "not the task of theology but of the obedience of faith."[79] It is the result of careful discernment and thorough Christian formation. Sharing possessions enables each individual and community to discern how God is calling them to use their gifts. Sharing provides a way to demonstrate God's love individually, congregationally, and globally.

---

78. Johnson, *Sharing Possessions*, 105.
79. Johnson, *Sharing Possessions*, 106.

3 ▪ What Does Scripture Say? Understanding the Theology of the Congregation

Chapter 2 discussed how the scripture supports various theological views on money. Clearly, one can find scriptural support for divergent views on faith and finance. In a recent survey of 211 self-identified Christians, 64 percent of the respondents identified Bible stories and teachings of Jesus that focused on money. The overwhelming majority of the respondents in a clergy survey also indicated that people in their congregations were aware of this biblical material. Since discussions of money can be hard to lead, those scriptural sources can provide one of the easiest ways for us to start to identify our personal theology of money, even if we do not believe that we have one. They also expose the underlying emotions in the congregation about money and the congregation's embedded theology of money.

This chapter examines some of the most consistently cited stories and teachings about money and what they may tell us about ourselves. In his book, *The Righteous Mind: Why Good People Are Divided by Politics and Religion*, social psychologist Jonathan Haidt argues that we make their decisions based on one of six "moral foundations:" authority/subversion, fairness/cheating, sanctity/degradation, liberty/oppression, care/harm, and loyalty/betrayal.

While we generally believe that we are making rational decisions, Haidt demonstrates that we actually make emotional decisions, and subsequently find intellectual justification for those decisions.[80] In analyzing scripture passages related to money, Haidt's framework is a useful tool for identifying the underlying emotions provoked by each passage. Using those emotions as a guide, we will be in the best position to understand our theology of money and to discern a way to address financial anxiety.

Authority

> He blessed him and said, "Blessed be Abram by God Most High, maker of heaven and earth; and blessed be God Most High, who has delivered your enemies into your hand!" And Abram gave him one-tenth of everything.
>
> Gen. 14:19–20

Genesis 14:19–20 provides one of the most explicit references to our use of resources, including money, in scripture. There are similar passages at Leviticus 27:30–32, and Numbers 18:21, 24, which describe the Levitical tithe, and Deuteronomy 14:22–27, which describes annual festival giving. Yet, according to Nonprofits Source, only 5 percent of Christians give a tithe, and on average, they are giving just 2.5 percent of their income. Even during the Great Depression, Americans tithed an average of 3.3 percent of

---

80. Jonathan Haidt, *The Righteous Mind: Why Good People Are Divided by Politics and Religion* (New York: Vantage Books, 2012), 29, 61.

their income.[81] Since tithing is so rare, what does it say if you cite this passage as an example of theology and money? How might it speak to financial anxiety?

Based on Haidt's analysis of moral foundations, people who cite tithing may be people who respond well to authority. They appreciate clear rules, and this passage provides clear financial guidance. Out of respect for the authority of the Bible and the authority of the Church, people who cite this verse might respond well to a theological discussion about money that focuses on authority. They may experience financial anxiety because they do not have the means to tithe at this time. Particularly during the COVID-19 pandemic and its aftermath, many people have not had the resources to tithe to their church. Therefore, a congregational leader might use her authority to assure parishioners that God is compassionate and slow to anger, including when people are unable to tithe. A leader might also want to lead a conversation about what authority is needed to change our personal budgets or the church budget. On its surface, this kind of conversation may seem merely procedural, but it might quickly reveal our emotions surrounding money, and provoke a theological discussion about financial anxiety. Do you feel powerless over their financial situation? Do you believe that they have the authority to change their behavior?

Conversely, someone citing this passage might not be particularly moved by Haidt's moral foundations of care and fairness.

---

81. "Charitable Giving for Churches," Nonprofits Source, https://nonprofitssource.com/online-giving-statistics/church-giving/.

This is not to say that those people do not value those moral foundations, but they might not respond to them as quickly as they do to authority. The goal of this exercise is to understand the moral foundations that are most important to each individual. Subsequently, we can seek out the appropriate care and support. Based on insights garnered from a Bible passage, a leader can chart a course for her congregation or an individual can chart a course for herself, which could lead to a theological discussion of money.

Fairness

The Beatitudes

Blessed are the poor in spirit, for theirs is the kingdom of heaven.

Blessed are those who mourn, for they will be comforted.

Blessed are the meek, for they will inherit the earth.

Blessed are those who hunger and thirst for righteousness, for they will be filled.

Blessed are the merciful, for they will receive mercy.

Blessed are the pure in heart, for they will see God.

Blessed are the peacemakers, for they will be called children of God.

Blessed are those who are persecuted for righteousness' sake, for theirs is the kingdom of heaven.

Blessed are you when people revile you and persecute you and utter all kinds of evil against you falsely on my account. Rejoice and be glad, for your reward is great in heaven, for in the same way they persecuted the prophets who were before you.

Matt. 5:3–12

For many Christians, the Beatitudes paint the perfect image of heaven; those who have suffered in this world will be rewarded in the next. People who cite this passage when referring to money are envisioning a world of tremendous fairness. Therefore, a theological discussion of financial anxiety could start with the value of fairness. Church leaders could start a conversation about income inequality or poverty, and that conversation might prompt congregants to explore their emotions about money. People might be invited to share the ways in which unfairness in the current economic system is affecting them and creating financial anxiety. Are they worried about losing health care or being evicted? What do the Beatitudes tell them about those concerns? Do Jesus's words provide any relief? Do they feel any solace in knowing that others also suffer from financial anxiety? The moral foundation of fairness can be a strong place to start talking about money.

> Then Jesus looked around and said to his disciples, "How hard it will be for those who have wealth to enter the kingdom of God!" And the disciples were perplexed at these words. But Jesus said to them again, "Children, how hard it is to enter the kingdom of God! It is easier for a camel to go through the eye of a needle than for someone who is rich to enter the kingdom of God." They were greatly astounded and said to one another, "Then who can be saved?" Jesus looked at them and said, "For mortals it is impossible, but not for God; for God all things are possible."
>
> Peter began to say to him, "Look, we have left everything and followed you." Jesus said, "Truly I tell you, there is no

one who has left house or brothers or sisters or mother or father or children or fields, for my sake and for the sake of the good news, who will not receive a hundredfold now in this age—houses, brothers and sisters, mothers and children, and fields, with persecutions—and in the age to come eternal life. But many who are first will be last, and the last will be first.

Mark 10:23–31

The story of the rich young man can disturb people. Is Jesus requiring everyone to sell everything to be his disciple? Not necessarily. Jesus did not require the disciples to sell everything. We know from scripture that they still had access to the house in Capernaum and to fishing boats. Typically, this passage is interpreted as one about individual discipleship. Jesus knew that the rich young man would never be able to follow him unless he sold his possessions. This story highlights that Jesus saw wealth as a potential peril. However, he did not see wealth as a peril for everyone and in every situation. Rather, Jesus insists on personal discipleship. He wants his disciples to be aware of those things that keep them from God. People who cite this passage may be concerned with fairness. Was it fair for Jesus to ask so much of the rich young man? What is God asking of them?

Since we cannot be entirely sure what God is asking of us, this story can evoke anxiety. To help address the anxiety, we might want to engage a discussion about what is fair for someone to possess. This could lead to the consideration of the virtue of sufficiency. A virtue of sufficiency presupposes that God's abundance is sufficient to take care of everyone as long as people are willing to share. What would be sufficient for us and what would it be like if we gave the rest of our money away? The challenge with this consideration is that "sufficiency" and "necessity" can mean very different things to different people. As a result, there may be a need to develop community standards for wealth and possessions. A congregation could establish some basic guidelines for money and sufficiency. In leading this conversation, a facilitator should be mindful that some critics worry that a virtue of sufficiency might undermine economic growth. Therefore, part of the discussion will need to focus on how sufficiency and economic growth can co-exist. Uncertainty can be a major source of financial anxiety. By discussing this passage, people may develop more clarity on what God is asking of them.

Cheating

He entered Jericho and was passing through it. A man was there named Zacchaeus; he was a chief tax collector and was rich. He was trying to see who Jesus was, but on account of the crowd he could not, because he was short in stature. So he ran ahead and climbed a sycamore tree to see him, because he was going to pass that way. When Jesus came to the place, he looked up and said to him, "Zacchaeus, hurry and come down; for I must stay at your house today." So he hurried down and was happy to welcome him. All who saw it began to grumble and said, "He has gone to be the guest of one who is a sinner." Zacchaeus stood there and said to the Lord, "Look, half of my possessions, Lord,

I will give to the poor; and if I have defrauded anyone of anything, I will pay back four times as much." Then Jesus said to him, "Today salvation has come to this house, because he too is a son of Abraham. For the Son of Man came to seek out and to save the lost."

Luke 19:1–10

The story of Zacchaeus is a wonderful account of redemption, and it reminds us that Jesus did not totally reject wealth, and he forgave those who cheated others. He recognized that wealth can be a blessing when used to serve others. This passage emphasizes the moral foundation of fairness and cheating. Zacchaeus repays the people that he cheated, and he dedicates half of his possessions to the poor. For those who cite this passage, a conversation about basic economic fairness could lead to a theological discussion of financial anxiety. How can we use our money in ways that are fair and in ways that help build equity? Are there local vendors that we could support that focus on fair practices and redemption? The Israelites considered the forgiveness of debt to be a form of redemption. Are there debts that we can forgive? If we advocate for a fairer and more forgiving economy, our advocacy might actually reduce our financial anxiety. Even if a more just and forgiving economy is far off, the prospect of and participation in creating change can be hopeful, and it can reduce anxiety.

Sanctity

Do not store up for yourselves treasures on earth, where moth and rust consume and where thieves break in and

> steal; but store up for yourselves treasures in heaven, where neither moth nor rust consumes and where thieves do not break in and steal. For where your treasure is, there your heart will be also.
>
> Matt. 6:19–21

This passage from Matthew appears routinely in the lectionary, and for those who cite it, they may prioritize Haidt's moral foundation of sanctity and have an aversion to degradation. They may have negative visceral reactions to money, which fuels their financial anxiety. Those who cite it might consider how they feel about money. Does it make them feel "dirty" or "bad"? If these individuals see money as dirty and bad, then it may not be surprising that they experience financial anxiety, regardless of how much money they have. As a result, we might ask ourselves how money could be made to feel "clean." Is there a way to redeem money?

Degradation

> For the love of money is a root of all kinds of evil, and in their eagerness to be rich some have wandered away from the faith and pierced themselves with many pains.
>
> 1 Tim. 6:10

This passage from 1 Timothy is frequently cited out of context and misquoted as "money is the root of all evil," rather than "the love of money is the root of all evil." 1 Timothy reflects both the potential for personal degradation and for the idolatry of money. The passage can also create a lot of financial confusion for Christians. If "money is the root of all evil," then how are we supposed to pay our bills and feed our families? Paul was not necessarily telling Christians to ignore their financial responsibilities, but to balance them with their love of God. People who cite this passage may respond to the moral foundation of sanctity/holiness. By focusing too much on money, we risk undermining sanctity because we make compromises for money that jeopardize our discipleship. This passage could provide a helpful way to discuss how God has called us to love. Jesus reminds his listeners to love God and one another. If we loved God and one another, what would that mean for how we use our money? What is the proper relationship for followers of Christ to have with money? Is there a way to use money without developing a love for it? This passage naturally leads into a theological discussion of financial anxiety. It clearly reflects the perils of money; so, it might be constructive to also discuss the obligations and responsibilities that come with money.

Liberty

For it is as if a man, going on a journey, summoned his slaves and entrusted his property to them; to one he gave five talents, to another two, to another one, to each according to his ability. Then he went away. The one who had received the five talents went off at once and traded with them, and made five more talents. In the same way, the one who had the two talents made two more talents. But the one who had received the one talent went off and dug a hole in the ground and hid his master's money. After a long time the master of those slaves came and settled accounts with them. Then the one who had received the five talents came forward, bringing five more talents, saying, 'Master, you handed over to me five talents; see, I have made five more talents.' His master said to him, 'Well done, good and trustworthy slave; you have been trustworthy in a few things, I will put you in charge of many things; enter into the joy of your master.' And the one with the two talents also came forward, saying, 'Master, you handed over to me two talents; see, I have made two more talents.' His master said to him, 'Well done, good and trustworthy slave; you have been trustworthy in a few things, I will put you in charge of many things; enter into the joy of your master.' Then the one who had received the one talent also came forward, saying, 'Master, I knew that you were a harsh man, reaping where you did not sow, and gathering where you did not scatter seed; so I was afraid, and I went and hid your talent in the ground. Here you have what is yours.' But his master replied, 'You wicked and lazy slave! You knew, did you, that I reap where I did not sow, and gather where I did not scatter? Then you ought to have invested my money with the bankers, and on my return, I would have received what was my own with interest. So, take the talent from him, and give it to the one with the ten talents. For to all those who have, more will be given, and they will have an abundance; but from those who have nothing, even what they have will be taken away. As for this worthless slave, throw him into the outer darkness, where there will be weeping and gnashing of teeth.

Matt. 25:14–30

This challenging passage has elicited a broad range of scriptural interpretations. Many people see individual liberty in this passage, since slaves made their own decisions about how they handled the master's money, and then, faced the consequences of their decisions. However, some commentators have argued that the slave who did not invest was actually criticizing the economic system by refusing to invest in it. Therefore, some people actually see oppression in this passage. The master is setting up an intensely competitive system between the slaves that ultimately oppresses them. Our current economic system rests heavily on competition. Jesus was an anti-rival who tried to move his disciples beyond competition. Frequently, in the United States, competition is justified as part of our meritocracy. In a meritocracy, it is assumed that the people with the best skills and abilities receive the best rewards. But, what does that mean for everyone else? People who see this system as fair may still find themselves on the losing end of it, and that can generate massive financial anxiety for them. Some people may believe that there is no way for them to win in the current economic system. In fact, for those people, the current system may be oppressive. For them, a theological discussion of meritocracy and the current economic system may be a very good way to help them to understand and cope with their financial anxiety.

Oppression

Come now, you rich people, weep and wail for the miseries that are coming to you. Your riches have rotted, and your clothes are moth-eaten. Your gold and silver have rusted, and their rust will be evidence against you, and it will eat your flesh like fire. You have laid up treasure for the last days. Listen! The wages of the laborers who mowed your fields, which you kept back by fraud, cry out, and the cries of the harvesters have reached the ears of the Lord of hosts. You have lived on the earth in luxury and in pleasure; you have fattened your hearts in a day of slaughter. You have condemned and murdered the righteous one, who does not resist you.

James 5:1–6

On its face, this passage appears to be highly critical of wealth, but James's message is more subtle. Rather, than condemning the rich, James is warning against fraud and corruption. People who cite this passage are likely to respond to the moral foundation of oppression. To alleviate financial anxiety, they may want to discuss fairness and sharing. Rather than just actively or passively participating in systems of oppression, people may find some relief if they are able to share their possessions, and encourage others to do the same.

Care

The apostles gathered around Jesus, and told him all that they had done and taught. He said to them, "Come away to a deserted place all by yourselves and rest a while." For many were coming and going, and they had no leisure even to eat. And they went away in the boat to a deserted place by themselves. Now many saw them going and recognized them, and they hurried there on foot from all the towns and arrived ahead of them. As he went ashore, he saw a great crowd; and he had compassion for them, because they were like sheep without a shepherd; and he began to teach them many things. When it grew late, his disciples came to him and said, "This is a deserted place, and the hour is now very late; send them away so that they may go into the surrounding country and villages and buy something for themselves to eat." But he answered them, "You give them something to eat." They said to him, "Are we to go and buy two hundred denarii worth of bread, and give it to them to eat?" And he said to them, "How many loaves have you? Go and see." When they had found out, they said, "Five, and two fish." Then he ordered them to get all the people to sit down in groups on the green grass. So, they sat down in groups of hundreds and of fifties. Taking the five loaves and the two fish, he looked up to heaven, and blessed and broke the loaves, and gave them to his disciples to set before the people; and he divided the two fish among them all. And all ate and were filled; and they took up twelve baskets full of broken pieces and of the fish. Those who had eaten the loaves numbered five thousand men.

Mark 6:30–44

People who cite the "Feeding of the 5,000" are likely to appreciate the abundance in God's world, and the way in which God and Jesus care for us. They will probably respond to caring as a basis for a conversation about financial anxiety. Therefore, it might be constructive for them to think about a time when they experienced scarcity. What did it feel like to be lacking, and where was God for them? For many people, the fear of scarcity is the primary driver of their financial anxiety. For this group, a theological conversation about financial anxiety could emerge from a focus on scarcity. What would it take for us to trust that God cares for us? Could renewed confidence in God's care reduce financial anxiety?

Harm

He said to his disciples, "Therefore I tell you, do not worry about your life, what you will eat, or about your body, what you will wear. For life is more than food, and the body more than clothing. Consider the ravens: they neither sow nor reap, they have neither storehouse nor barn, and yet God feeds them. Of how much more value are you than the birds! And can any of you by worrying add a single hour to your span of life? If then you are not able to do so small a thing as that, why do you worry about the rest? Consider the lilies, how they grow: they neither toil nor spin; yet I tell you, even Solomon in all his glory was not clothed like one of these. But if God so clothes the grass of the field, which is alive today and tomorrow is thrown into the oven, how much more will he clothe you—you of little faith! And do not keep striving for what you are to eat and what you are to drink, and do not keep worrying. For it is the nations of the world that strive after all these things, and your Father knows that you need them. Instead, strive for his kingdom, and these things will be given to you as well.

> Do not be afraid, little flock, for it is your Father's good pleasure to give you the kingdom. Sell your possessions, and give alms. Make purses for yourselves that do not wear out, an unfailing treasure in heaven, where no thief comes near and no moth destroys. For where your treasure is, there your heart will be also.
>
> Luke 12:22–34

When asked about money and scripture, many people cite this passage from Luke. Those who cite it might wish that they could trust in God in the ways Jesus suggests. Jesus implies that individuals need not worry about possessions in this life because God will care for them. However, many people are understandably too anxious to trust Jesus's words completely. It would seem naïve to ignore the potential harm in the world. They recognize that God expects us to exercise some responsibility for our self-care. When quoting Deuteronomy, Jesus said "Do not put the Lord your God to the test" (Matt. 4:7 NRSV). For many, it seems that they would be putting God to the test if they expected God to provide for all of their material needs.

To fully understand this passage, it helps to look at all of Luke chapter 12. At the beginning of chapter 12, Jesus discusses appropriate and inappropriate fears (Luke 12:4–7 NRSV). After this passage, Jesus describes the rewards or punishments that come from sharing our possessions (Luke 12:35–48 NRSV).[82] While

---

82. Ely Wheeler, *Wealth as Peril and Obligation*, 67.

people tend to focus on verses 22 to 34, Jesus provides this guidance within a much greater context. He is encouraging fearlessness, and he wants his followers to recognize that what they pursue in their lives is what they treasure. Reading all of chapter 12 might make it easier to understand Jesus's message. Jesus understood financial anxiety, and based on his directives, he wanted us to do something about it. He hoped that we would choose faith before finances.

For many Christians who struggle to follow Jesus's advice, financial anxiety can be debilitating. Psychologists believe that our culture is increasingly addicted to anxiety, and that it is fueling addiction to drugs and alcohol.[83] Luke 12:22–34 is aspirational for many people. It also may reflect an emphasis on authority. What if God actually exercised the authority to take care of all your needs? Because God gives us free will, God does not intercede as directly as we might like, and yet God is still abundantly present in our lives. This passage may provide an opportunity to raise questions of how faith can alleviate financial anxiety. What could Christians pursue instead of money? In his ministry, Jesus provides several suggestions: prayer, care for the poor, welcoming others. Modern psychologists recommend some of these same tools as ways to alleviate anxiety. Ultimately, Jesus directed his disciples to

---

83. Judith Orloff, M.D., "Are You Addicted to Anxiety? Lean How Not to Be," *Psychology Today*, April 11, 2011. https://www.psychologytoday.com /us/blog/emotional-freedom/201104/are-you-addicted-anxiety-learn-how -not-be.

focus on God, rather than money. Could such a profound shift in focus reduce societal financial anxiety? Jesus and the psychologists seem to agree that it could.

Loyalty

> He sat down opposite the treasury, and watched the crowd putting money into the treasury. Many rich people put in large sums. A poor widow came and put in two small copper coins, which are worth a penny. Then he called his disciples and said to them, "Truly I tell you, this poor widow has put in more than all those who are contributing to the treasury. For all of them have contributed out of their abundance; but she out of her poverty has put in everything she had, all she had to live on."
>
> Mark 12:41–44

The story of the widow's copper coins is an example of tremendous loyalty. The poor widow gives everything that she has to the temple. People who are drawn to this passage might prioritize exceptional loyalty. They may benefit from reflecting on times in their lives when they felt intensely loyal. Conversely, have they ever experienced betrayal? Have they ever felt intense loyalty to the church? What does it look like to be loyal to God? Is loyalty to the church a different thing from loyalty to God? Does loyalty to God require an exceptional financial sacrifice, like the widow's?

Loyalty also can be a source of financial anxiety. People may feel obligated to maintain a strong financial commitment to others or organizations to demonstrate their loyalty. As a result, their loyalty can bring with it financial pressure, which can easily turn to anxiety. For example, parents may feel the need to buy their children everything that they ask for to demonstrate loyalty and commitment to them. However, loyalty and financial commitment are not the same as love. It might be helpful for parents to remember the distinction between wants and needs. Chapter 1 described the ways in which mimetic desire causes people to confuse wants with needs. As a result, we might consider the following question: Can we remain loyal without providing financial support?

This passage also seems to imply that people should give all their money to the church. In that way, the passage echoes the story of the rich young ruler. It seems to suggest that money is a potential peril. Is there a way to develop a healthy relationship with money while still demonstrating loyalty to the people and institutions that are important to us? Developing a healthy relationship with money is essential for managing financial anxiety.

Betrayal

> Then Jesus entered the temple and drove out all who were selling and buying in the temple, and he overturned the tables of the money changers and the seats of those who sold doves. He said to them, "It is written, 'My house shall be called a house of prayer'; but you are making it a den of robbers."
>
> Matt. 21:12–13

Jesus's famous "cleansing of the temple" during Holy Week might be one of the strongest cases for sanctity, but for those who cite it, this passage also demonstrates betrayal. Jesus objected to the moneychangers because they were cheating the pilgrims who came to Jerusalem. As a result, they desecrated God's house and betrayed God's trust. Pilgrims would journey to Jerusalem, and if they wanted to make an offering, they needed to buy the animal to offer and then give the animal to the temple priests. Moneychangers were necessary, but the moneychangers took advantage of God's people. As a result, this passage could provoke a discussion about economic inequality. Are there ways that we might address cheating that occurs within our communities? This passage could also spark a conversation about activities that might betray the church and betray our faith. Are there modern equivalents of moneychangers?

4 ▪ What Are We to Do?

Starting a theological discussion about financial anxiety is hard. When money is discussed in church, people usually think about stewardship. I have led many conversations about money in church, and people always revert to stewardship. A theological discussion of financial anxiety can be easier when a congregation has a more comprehensive understanding of the emotions surrounding money. The Bible passages listed in chapter 3 can reveal a great deal about the emotions surrounding money that individuals and congregations may have internalized without realization. Money and financial anxiety need to become a normalized part of our faith discussion, just like death, illness, and sexuality. Chapter 4 offers some tools to start those conversations. While these tools do not necessarily cover financial anxiety directly, they start a conversation about money that can ultimately lead to a conversation about financial anxiety.

Chapter 4 presents two pastoral curricula. The first curriculum focuses on individual budgeting, and the second focuses on congregational investing. They are both four-week programs that include coffee-hour forums and group exercises/experiments. The group exercises and experiments are the primary focus. These exercises and experiments offer an alternative approach to a theological discussion of financial anxiety. Ultimately, participants will be developing new "habits" for their money: their own "Rule of Life" for money. More importantly, the curricula empower leaders to develop their own exercises and experiments that would be most effective in their contexts. Talking theologically about financial anxiety will require adaptive changes to our congregations. These exercises offer some technical fixes that can launch theological conversations and ultimately result in adaptive changes.

Program One: Making Budgets Holy

The first program focuses on personal budgeting. Proper budgeting can help address financial anxiety. This program seeks to expose the beliefs and behaviors that make it difficult for people to set and maintain budgets. For many people, living within their means is impossible. Nevertheless, budgeting provides a way of controlling one's money, rather than being controlled by it, even for people who do not have enough money to achieve a balanced budget. More important, a theological discussion of budgets can assure people that God is in everything, even their budgets, and they can make their budgets holy.

Week One: Budgeting Introduction and "Money Memoir"

On page 445 of the Book of Common Prayer, it says:

The Minister of the Congregation is directed to instruct the people, from time to time, about the duty of Christian parents to make prudent provisions for the well-being of their families.[84]

---

84. *The Book of Common Prayer* (New York, NY: Oxford University Press, 2007), 445.

While this rubric has largely been applied to wills and estates, it also suggests that parents must maintain a basic level of budgeting and financial planning for the well-being of their children. We celebrate the Feast of St. Matthew, the patron of financial matters, on September 21. In the Lord's Prayer, we ask God to "forgive us our debts, as we forgive our debtors," and the original Greek translation contemplated monetary and non-monetary debts. All three point to the importance of budgeting and financial management within the history of the church. During the first week of this pastoral program, a personal financial planner will present the basics of personal financial management during a Sunday forum. During the following week, people will be encouraged to keep track of all of their spending. They will also be encouraged to keep a "money memoir."[85] In a money memoir, a person writes about memories of money. The money memoir is like a personal journal; it is not meant to be shared with others. Dr. Kate Levinson, a psychotherapist who specializes in money issues, has found that writing a money memoir is one of the most effective ways for working through individuals' issues around money. In many cases, a money memoir is a necessary first step before people can even begin to talk about financial anxiety. During the upcoming week, program participants will be asked to record their emotions over keeping track of their spending and the prospects of maintaining a budget.

---

85. Kate Levinson, *Emotional Currency: A Woman's Guide to Building a Healthy Relationship with Money* (Berkeley, CA: Celestial Arts, 2011), 41–53.

Week Two: Money Lifestyles

The forum for the second week will encourage people to think about their own lifestyles and the ways in which their lifestyles reflect their faith. As part of this exercise, there will be an introduction to developing a "rule for money." This exercise has been developed from "A Framework for Rule-Crafting Practice," introduced by Jane Patterson and Steven Tomlinson at Seminary of the Southwest.[86] Patterson and Tomlinson suggest that habits are anchored in the core assumptions and the unspoken biases of our lives. At times, those habits can limit or even contradict our beliefs. Therefore, they suggest looking at one small habit in our life, and examining its consequences to our faith. They frame this thought experiment with a matrix considering one's behavior and belief in the present situation and one's behavior and belief as a future possibility. This rule-crafting practice can clarify the discernment process and ultimately, it can help people to develop new habits.

	The Present	The Possibility
Behavior		
Belief		

Patterson and Tomlinson explain the use of this matrix with the following example. Mark is a man who feels sluggish and foggy most of the time, because he only sleeps four hours per night.

---

86. Jane Patterson and Steven Tomlinson, "A Framework for Rule-Crafting Practice." Seminary of the Southwest, 2018, p 1.

Using the rule-crafting matrix, they can guide Mark through a discernment about his sleep patterns and they ultimately lead him through a theological discussion of sleep. The exercise starts with the present behavior. Mark sleeps only four hours per night.

	The Present	The Possibility
Behavior	Sleeps about four hours/night	
Belief		

Then, the matrix challenges Mark to identify the belief that supports that habit. Mark concludes that sleep is a waste of time. Mark also knows that he feels sluggish and foggy most of the time. The exercise challenges him to consider what it might be like if he permitted himself more sleep. He realizes that it is possible that he could feel rested and refreshed. After careful discernment Mark identifies his underlying belief, and he considers a different possible behavior.

	The Present	The Possibility
Behavior	Sleeps about four hours/night	I could be rested, refreshed
Belief	Sleep is a waste of time	

After identifying his underlying belief and the possibility of a change in his behavior, Mark can examine overlooked aspects of his beliefs or entirely new beliefs that would support the new possibility. For example, rather than viewing sleep as a waste of time, Mark could view it as a gift from God.

	The Present	The Possibility
Behavior	Sleeps about four hours/night	I could be rested, refreshed
Belief	Sleep is a waste of time	Sleep is a gift from God

In this exercise, Mark has been able to identify a limiting belief, that is, "Sleep is a waste of time." As long as he continues to see sleep as a waste of time, he will not change his habit. But, if Mark started to see sleep's refreshing properties as a gift from God, then he might be able to change his habit. Ultimately, after reflecting on all of these beliefs and behaviors, Mark may conclude that "Each night when I finally lie down to sleep, I will offer a prayer of thanks for the gift and accept it graciously."[87] As a result of the rule-crafting exercise, Mark can change his behavior and develop a new rule for this life. This same "rule-crafting practice," can be applied to any area of life. For this pastoral program, we will be using it to discern new rules for our money.

In the upcoming week, people will be encouraged to consider some of their rules around money. They could write about these rules in their money memoirs, and next Sunday, the group will run the rule-crafting practice to develop some money rules for themselves.[88] They could also use this matrix to examine some of their current money beliefs and behaviors. For example, they might want to consider the challenge between their desire for security and their belief in sharing with others. They might start with a belief that

---

87. Jane Patterson and Steven Tomlinson, "A Framework," 9.
88. Jane Patterson and Steven Tomlinson, "A Framework," 4–6.

they must provide for their family, and then identify the resulting behavior. They might also consider sharing their resources with others. After discernment and prayer during the week, individuals might start to see new possibilities for their behavior. Working through the rule-crafting practice on their own will prepare them for the next week, when the group will work on this exercise together.

	The Present	The Possibility
Behavior	Prioritizing personal security	
Belief	I must provide for my family	Sharing vs. Idolatry

Participants might also want to consider the challenge for them in budgeting. They might start by looking at their spending habits. For example, maybe they spend every paycheck and they are unable to put aside any savings. Based on their behavior, their underlying belief seems to be that there is never enough money to go around.

	The Present	The Possibility
Behavior	Spend every paycheck	
Belief	There is never enough	

However, this belief might contradict the numerous times that Jesus tells people that there is more than enough for everyone. For example, Jesus said, "Therefore I tell you, do not worry about your life, what you will eat, or about your body, what you will wear. For life is more than food, and the body more than clothing" (Luke 12:22 NRSV) What would it look like to the forum participants if they really trusted in what Jesus says in Luke 12:22? Would it change their behavior? Could they make saving part of their money habit because they could be confident that their needs would be taken care of? Could they cut some expenses in their budget to be sure that they could save some money every week?

	The Present	The Possibility
Behavior	Spend every paycheck	
Belief	There is never enough	Luke 12:22

This is a very sensitive area for people. Given the high cost of housing in most metropolitan areas in the United States, housing costs may be the reason that people are unable to keep a budget, which could lead to an entirely different matrix. Depending on the ministry's context, it might be best to start with the behavior that forces housing to take the majority of people's incomes. They would start with their current behavior.

	The Present	The Possibility
Behavior	Majority of income on rent	
Belief		

This exercise will help them to explore that behavior. What belief is holding them to that behavior? Are they worried about their safety if they live in a different neighborhood? Are they trying to get the best education for their children? The matrix will help them to see their present beliefs, and consider whether those beliefs are consistent with their desired beliefs and the possible behaviors that they could change. Perhaps they could embrace the virtue of sufficiency suggested by Thomas Aquinas and Msgr. John Ryan, SJ. Are they worried about things that are not necessary for their subsistence? What constitutes "sufficiency" for them? Would a "sufficient" budget leave them with some money to save?

	The Present	The Possibility
Behavior	Majority of income on rent	
Belief		Virtue of Sufficiency

Patterson and Tomlinson give another example of rule-crafting that could be applied to money. In this example, a woman is challenged by Jesus's command to "give to everyone who begs from you" (Luke 6:30 NRSV), and what that might actually look like in her life.[89] Therefore, in her case, she started her discernment with the possibility of living out that gospel directive.

	The Present	The Possibility
Behavior		"Give to everyone who asks"
Belief		

In her discernment, she discovers that her family had a deep concern about scarcity. Her parents were always afraid that they

---

89. Jane Patterson and Steven Tomlinson, "A Framework," 6–8.

would not have enough to support their family. Her family taught her that there was not enough for everyone; so, they needed to guard their resources. Understandably, her family's fear of scarcity shaped her beliefs. Because of a fear of scarcity, she discovered that she was not even listening to homeless people that approached her on the street. She assumed that they would want money from her, which she did not have to give to them.

	The Present	The Possibility
Behavior	Not listening, even before an ask	"Give to everyone who asks"
Belief	Things are scarce; there is not enough	

In discernment, she began to consider how to reconcile her behavior and beliefs with Jesus's possibility. She realized that she immediately turned away from strangers, even before they asked her anything. She resolved to take a risk and at least listen to the people approaching her.

As she started to listen to more people, she discovered that most people did not actually want money from her. Many simply needed someone to acknowledge them and listen to them. As a result, she concluded that, in fact, she did have enough to share with everyone who asked her.

	The Present	The Possibility
Behavior	Not listening, even before an ask	"Give to everyone who asks"
Belief	Things are scarce; there is not enough	I have enough to share

She developed a new rule for herself. "I will give my attention to everyone who asks."[90] In this case, what began as a concern about scarcity and money turned into a habit of openness and abundance. This week, people will adopt that same process to consider their approaches to money. Is there a belief or habit that is inconsistent with the possibilities described by Jesus? What does "giving to everyone" mean to them? Would these new rules reduce their financial anxiety?

Week Three: Making Budgets

For Week Three, the program exercise will build on the prior week's rule-crafting practice, but this week the rule-crafting will relate specifically to budgets. This week's forum starts by using the rule-crafting matrix to consider the possibility of a belief in having a balanced budget. What are the possible changes in behavior that might enable the forum participants to have a balanced budget? Are there any unnecessary expenses in their weekly spending? Could debts be consolidated? As a result of this analysis, what are the new money rules that are being generated for them?

	The Present	The Possibility
Behavior	Unbalanced budget	
Belief	Maintain a balanced budget	

---

90. Jane Patterson and Steven Tomlinson, "A Framework," 10.

How could this new money rule change their life? How might it impact their faith? Would it reduce their financial anxiety and possibly increase their faith? Perhaps the participants could consider Matthew 6:25, "Therefore I tell you, do not worry about your life, what you will eat or what you will drink, or about your body, what you will wear. Is not life more than food, and the body more than clothing?" If they had a balanced budget, would they worry less, as suggested by Jesus? Could they also develop greater financial confidence?

	The Present	The Possibility
Behavior	Unbalanced budget	Financial Confidence
Belief	Maintain a balanced budget	Matthew 6:25–26

Again, this is a very sensitive topic, and provisions must be made to protect privacy and confidentiality. As difficult as this topic may be, people will be more likely to address it in the trusting community of their local congregation. If they are not able to trust their congregation, that might prompt different discernment and discussion. The congregation might consider another matrix and additional reflections in their money memoirs. What would it take for them to feel safe discussing money and their financial anxiety in their congregation? The goal of this exercise is not to get everyone to a balanced budget, but for everyone to see that their faith can address their finances and their financial anxiety.

Week Four: Trinity and Financial Anxiety

The final forum will seek to build on the work of the last three weeks and to make a more explicitly theological connection. The group will discuss the Trinity, and what a Trinitarian approach to personal spending and budgeting would look like. The facilitator would provide an overview of the concept of the Trinity as Creator, Redeemer, and Sustainer, rather than exclusively as Father, Son, and Holy Spirit. The Trinity is also a community of three persons (Father, Son, and Holy Spirit) that live in perfect unity together without competition or rivalry. The group will discuss what it would mean for personal spending to be creative, redemptive, and sustaining. Again, using the rule-crafting matrix the group will start by examining their current beliefs in the Trinity, and the possibility of believing in the Trinity as Creator, Redeemer and Sustainer.

	The Present	The Possibility
Behavior		
Belief	Father, Son, and Holy Spirit	Creator, Redeemer, and Sustainer

Then, the group will examine whether their current belief in the Trinity is affecting their personal spending. Perhaps they are not connecting their purchases to God or the Trinity at all. What would happen if they prioritized purchases that were creative, redemptive, and sustaining? For example, instead of buying coffee at a national chain, perhaps they could find a local coffee shop that uses its space to support local artists and local community initiatives.

	The Present	The Possibility
Behavior		Creative, redemptive, and sustaining purchases
Belief	Father, Son, and Holy Spirit	Creator, Redeemer, and Sustainer

The group could also consider the spending implications from considering the Trinity to be a community. If God lives in perfect community of the Father, Son, and Holy Spirit, what would it look like to prioritize purchases that reflect a community of all God's people? Are there communal ways of organizing spending? Are there ways of participating in the economy that reduce competition, rivalry, and envy? Perhaps participants could prioritize shopping at a local farmers market that offers products by local farmers and local food producers, rather than shopping at a major grocery store chain. Maybe they could seek to work with a local bank or credit union.

	The Present	The Possibility
Behavior		Farmers' market
Belief	Father, Son, and Holy Spirit	Community of Three Persons of God

As this program wraps up, there is the opportunity for the individuals in the program to continue to consider their faith in their purchases and their budgets. Members may want to continue to meet, so that they can work together to determine what are creative, redemptive, and sustaining purchases. They may want to collectively discern a virtue of sufficiency. In the past, people have been most successful at connecting their faith with their purchases and money, when they have discussed these ideas in community. The Acts of the Apostles and monastic communities have openly discussed and shared their resources. From this discernment process, people can continually evaluate their budgets and their faith. In addition, this exercise provides a community conversation about financial anxiety. As a result, an ongoing theological discussion of money and financial anxiety can continue long after this program is completed. The group can both support and guide each other in the challenges of living with a budget that is consistent with one's faith.

Program Two: Making Investing Holy

The second pastoral program considers socially responsible investing. Socially responsible investing is difficult to define briefly, but it generally differs from traditional investing in three ways. First, it considers which investments should be excluded from a portfolio. Second, it considers how much advocacy the investors would like to have over the companies in which they invest. Third, investors consider the community impact of their investments.[91] Not every congregation has money invested or has savings; this exercise may not be as appropriate in those settings. These materials can also be applied to individual investing. For some congregations, a focus on individual investing may be more relevant than a focus on personal budgeting.

---

91. James W. Murphy, ed. *Faithful Investing: The Power of Decisive Action and Incremental Change* (New York: Church Publishing, 2019), 12.

Week One: Socially Responsible Investing

The first week of this program focuses on the fundamentals of socially responsible investing. The congregation's treasurer would hand out copies of the congregation's current balance sheet and investment portfolio, and provide a quick overview. Then, an investment advisor, or member of the church's investment committee, would describe the church's current investment strategy. The investment advisor would also provide an overview of socially responsible investing. Generally, socially responsible investing considers which investments should be excluded from a portfolio, investor activism, and impact investing in a community.[92] The group conversation would consider the following questions:

1. What are things that the congregation does not want to be invested in?

2. How much advocacy do they want to exercise over their investments? Are they willing to monitor the companies' decisions and raise objections at companies' annual meetings?

3. Are there community investments that they would like to make that could have an impact locally?

During the upcoming week, people will again be encouraged to use their money memoirs to reflect on the congregation's investments and potential money rules for the congregation, as well as for themselves.

---

92. Murphy, ed. *Faithful Investing*, 12.

Week Two: Rules for Investing

The second week of this program focuses on the congregation's follow-ups on the investment priorities from the prior week. But, this week, the group will use Patterson and Tomlinson's rule-crafting matrix. The conversation starts with the belief that the church wants to get the best return on its investments. Many vestries and investment committees believe that it is their fiduciary duty to secure the best possible investment returns for the congregation. Presumably, that belief would be reflected in the current investment portfolio.

	The Present	The Possibility
Behavior	Current portfolio	
Belief	Get the best return on investment	

This exercise might encourage them to think about a different belief. What if they tried to get a good return from socially responsible investing? Would they have to sacrifice investment performance? Not necessarily. According to KLD Indexes, from 2009 to 2019, the annualized returns for socially responsible investment funds was 10.63 percent compared to a 10.17 percent for the S&P 500.[93]

---

93. Shauna Carther Heyford, "Socially Responsible Mutual Funds," *Investopedia*, June 25, 2019. https://www.investopedia.com/articles /mutualfund/03/030503.asp#:~:text=According%20to%20KLD%20 Indexes%2C%20the,return%20from%20the%20S%26P%20500.

	The Present	The Possibility
Behavior	Current portfolio	Add socially responsible funds
Belief	Get the best return on investment	Get a socially responsible return

If the congregation prioritized socially responsible investing, then they might want to adjust their investment portfolio and include some socially responsible mutual funds in their portfolio. As a result, the congregation might begin to develop a new money rule for the congregation: socially responsible mutual funds.

Again, during the week, people will be encouraged to write in their money memoirs about the experience of developing this money rule, and they would also be encouraged to consider what socially responsible investing might mean for their own investing and personal spending.

Week Three: Impact Investing

The third week of the program will consider a different aspect of socially responsible investing: impact investing. What would it look like if the congregation made investments that had an impact on the local community? Instead of just investing in socially responsible mutual funds, the congregation could consider investing in some micro-lending programs that make small loans to low-income entrepreneurs who are starting businesses in their communities. Microfinance was pioneered by Muhammad Yunus at Grameen Bank in Bangladesh when he was trying to develop a credit delivery program for the rural poor in Bangladesh. It has been amazingly successful globally, and it has brought billions in capital to low-income people around the world. With these loans, people have started new businesses that have generated billions in new revenue and new opportunities. Therefore, instead of just securing the best returns or maintaining the current portfolio, the congregation might think about impact investing.

	The Present	The Possibility
Behavior	Current portfolio	
Belief	Get the best return on investment	Get an impactful return on investment

If the congregation could agree on getting an impactful return, then it could start to consider all the different ways in which it might change its investing behavior. When people start to see that investing can have a positive social impact, then they might have more confidence that the community would help them, too, if they got into financial trouble, which could alleviate their financial anxiety.

Week Four: Trinity and Investing

The final forum will build on the work of the last three weeks, and seek to make a more explicitly theological connection. The group discussion might focus on the Trinity, and what a Trinitarian investment strategy would look like. The Trinity is also a community of three persons (Father, Son, and Holy Spirit) that live in perfect unity together. What if the group sought investments that did the same? The group might discuss what it would mean for investments to be creative, redemptive, and sustaining and what it could mean to find investments that support the entire community. Again, using the rule-crafting matrix the group will start by examining their current belief in the Trinity, and the possibility of believing in the Trinity as Creator, Redeemer, and Sustainer.

	The Present	The Possibility
Behavior		
Belief	Father, Son, and Holy Spirit	Creator, Redeemer, and Sustainer

Then, the group will examine whether their current belief in the Trinity is a consideration in the congregation's investment strategy. Perhaps the congregation is deferring to investment advisors in the same way that they defer to a patriarchal notion of God the Father in the Trinity. What would happen if the congregation prioritized investments that were creative, redemptive, and sustaining?

	The Present	The Possibility
Behavior	Defer to authority	Creative, redemptive, and sustaining investments
Belief	Father, Son, and Holy Spirit	Creator, Redeemer, and Sustainer

The group could also consider the investment implications from considering the Trinity to be a community. If God lives in perfect community, what would it look like for congregational investments to reflect a community of all God's people? Perhaps, a communal view of the Trinity reinforces the need for the congregation to try impact investing. The discussion of communal responsibility would also return to sharing resources, which might also help alleviate financial anxiety.

	The Present	The Possibility
Behavior	Defer to authority	Community, impact investments
Belief	Father, Son, and Holy Spirit	Community of Three Persons of God

As this program wraps up, there is an opportunity for the congregation to continue to play a more active role in its investments. In particular, the congregation might want to set aside a portion of its portfolio for investments in impactful community investments that are creative, redemptive, and sustaining. For example, there may be a local small business that needs investors. The congregation could support a local coffee shop that provides creative space for local artists while also serving sustainable, fair trade coffee that employs people who have been recently incarcerated or recently arrived in the United States. Putting faith into action in investments is a good way to continue a theological discussion of money and to allay financial anxiety.

Conclusion

In a sermon at Christ Church Cathedral in Nashville, Tennessee, in 2013, then-presiding bishop of the Episcopal Church Katharine Jefferts Schori noted the tremendous difficulty that we have talking about money in the church, noting that many people see the topic of money as "the third rail."[94] Yet, a healthy conversation about money is essential for healthy congregations; but more importantly, it is essential for healthy congregants. Therefore, congregational leaders need to know how to talk about money, particularly how to lead a theological discussion of financial anxiety. Fortunately, the church has been discussing money and providing guidance on it for millennia, both in scripture and in theology. Congregational leaders have resources to lead this conversation. This book has attempted to provide the theological and scriptural basis for a discussion of financial anxiety and to provide some sample curricula for congregational leaders to start a theological discussion of money and financial anxiety. But this is only one approach to this topic. Any theological discussion of financial anxiety must reflect the congregational leaders' own setting. Therefore, leaders will need to discern how they can provide financial leadership in their own context and from their own backgrounds and experiences. In addition, leaders may face some resistance when leading

---

94. "Presiding bishop's sermon at Christ Church Cathedral, Nashville." Episcopaldigitalnetwork.com. http://episcopaldigitalnetwork.com/ens /2013/09/22/presiding-bishops-sermon-at-christ-church-cathedral-

a theological discussion of money. Many people come to church to be comforted and a theological discussion on financial anxiety might not be very comforting. However, as Levinson has seen in her practice, people are incredibly comforted once they start to face and name the complex set of emotions that they have about money.[95] Leaders will need to continually remind their congregations of the spiritual and theological importance of this work. Ultimately, our money does not need to hinder us. It can help to transform us, moving us past our financial anxieties, connecting us more fully in each other in the body of Christ, and building up God's beloved community.

---

95. Levinson, *Emotional Currency*, 2–10.

Bibliography

Allen, Pauline. "Challenges in Approaching Patristic Texts from the Perspective of Contemporary Catholic Social Teaching." In *Reading Patristic Texts on Social Ethics*, edited by Johan Leemans, Brian J. Matz, and Johan Verstraeten, 30–42. Washington, DC: Catholic University of America Press, 2011.

Althaus-Reid, Marcella. *Indecent Theology: Theological Perversions in Sex, Gender and Politics.* London: Routledge, 2000.

Bieringer, Reimund. "Texts that Create a Future." In Leemans, Matz, and Verstraeten, eds., 3–29.

Boff, Leonardo and Clodovis Boff. *Introduction to Liberation Theology.* Translated by Paul Burns. Maryknoll, NY: Orbis, 2016.

Brown, Brené. *The Gifts of Imperfection: Let Go of Who You Think You're Supposed to Be and Embrace Who You Are.* Center City, MN: Hazelden Publishing, 2010.

Brown, Eric. "Aristotle on the Choice of Lives: Two Concepts of Self-Sufficiency." Washington University, 4. http://www.artsci.wustl.edu/~eabrown/pdfs/Brown Autarkeia.pdf.

Brueggemann, Walter. *Journey to the Common Good.* Louisville, KY: Westminster John Knox Press, 2010.

_____ *Money and Possessions.* Louisville, KY: Westminster John Knox Press, 2016.

Busette, Camille. "Tax Reform in the Age of Inequality." *The Brookings Institute*, October 2, 2017. https://www.brookings.edu/blog/fixgov/2017/10/02/tax -reform-in-the-age-of-inequality/.

Cavanaugh, William T. *Being Consumed: Economics and Christian Desire.* Grand Rapids, MI: Eerdmans, 2008.

Christoffersen, John. "Rising inequality 'most important problem,' says Nobel-winning economist." *St. Louis Post-Dispatch*, October 14, 2013. http://www .stltoday.com/business/local/rising-inequality-most-important-problem-says -nobel-winning-economist/article_a5065957-05c3-5ac0-ba5b-dab91c22973a .html.

De La Torre, Miguel A. *Reading the Bible from the Margins.* Maryknoll, NY: Orbis Books, 2002.

Dropkin, Murray, Jim Halpin and Bill La Touche. *The Budget-Building Book for Nonprofits: A Step-by-Step Guide for Managers and Boards*. San Francisco, CA: John Wiley & Sons, 2007.

Durham, John. *Word Biblical Commentary: Exodus*. Grand Rapids, MI: Zondervan, 1987.

Dussel, Enrique. *Beyond Philosophy: Ethics, History, Marxism and Liberation Theology*. Edited by Eduardo Medieta. Lanham, MD: Rowman and Littlefield, 2003.

Ellacuria, Ignacio. *Ignacio Ellacuria: Essays on History, Liberation and Salvation*. Edited by Michael Lee. Maryknoll, NY: Orbis Press, 2013.

Ellul, Jacques. *Money and Power*. Downer Grove, IL: Inter-Varsity Press, 1984.

Facundo, Alvarado. "Inequality Over the Past Century," *International Monetary Fund*, September 2011. https://www.imf.org/external/pubs/ft/fandd/2011/09/picture.htm.

Firer Hinze, Christine. "What is Enough? Catholic Social Thought, Consumption, and Material Sufficiency." In *Having: Property and Possession in Religious and Social Life*, edited by William Schweiker, Charles Matthews, 162–188. Grand Rapids, MI: William B. Eerdmans Publishing Company, 2004.

Foster, Richard J. *Celebration of Discipline: The Path to Spiritual Growth*, Special Anniversary ed. New York: HarperOne, 2018.

Friedman, Edwin H. *A Failure of Nerve*, 10th anniversary rev. ed., edited Margaret M. Treadwell and Edward W. Beal. New York: Church Publishing, 2017.

Gebara, Ivone. *Longing for Running Water: Ecofeminism and Liberation*. Minneapolis, MN: Fortress Press, 1999.

Gonzalez, Justo L. *Faith and Wealth: A History of Early Christian Ideas on the Origin, Significance, and Use of Money*. Eugene, OR: Wipf and Stock Publishers, 2002.

Goodchild, Philip. *Theology of Money*. Durham, NC: Duke University Press, 2009.

Guttierez, Gustavo. *A Theology of Liberation*. Rev. ed. Edited and translated by Sister Caridad Inda and John Eagleson. Maryknoll, NY: Orbis Press, 2014.

Harlan, Beckley. "Theology and Prudence in John Ryan's Economic Ethics." In *Religion and Public Life: The Legacy of Monsignor John A. Ryan*, edited by Robert G. Kennedy, Mary Christine Athans, Bernard V. Brady, William C. McDonough, and Michael J. Naughton, 5–10. Lanham, MD: University Press of America, 2001.

Heifetz, Ronald and Marty Linsky. *Leadership on the Line: Staying Alive Through the Dangers of Change*. Boston, MA: Harvard Business Review Press, 2017.

Jefferts Schori, Katherine. "Presiding bishop's sermon at Christ Church Cathedral, Nashville." Episcopaldigitalnetwork.com. http://episcopaldigitalnetwork .com/ens/2013/09/22/presiding-bishops-sermon-at-christ-church-cathedral -nashville.

——————— "Values and Skills for Purpose," Trinity Cathedral, Phoenix, AZ, September 21, 2010. http://day1.org/2376-the_most_rev_katharine_jefferts _schori_values_and_skills_for_a_purpose/comments.

Johnson, Luke Timothy. *Sharing Possessions: What Faith Demands, 2nd ed.* Grand Rapids, MI: Eerdmans, 2011.

Keucher, Gerald W., *Remember the Future: Financial Leadership and Asset Management for Congregations*. New York, NY: Church Publishing, 2006.

Krueger, David A. "Can John Ryan's Economic Ethic Work for a Global Economy." In Kennedy, Athans, Brady, McDonough, and Naughton, eds., 197–210.

Leemans, Johan and John Verstraeten. "The (Im)possible Dialogue between Patristic and Catholic Social Thought." In Leemans, Matz, and Verstraeten, eds., 222–231.

Leonhardt, Megan. "75% of millennial couples talk about money at least once a week–and it seems to be working for them," CNBC.com, July 31, 2018. https://www.cnbc.com/2018/07/27/75-percent-of-millennial-couples-talk -about-money-at-least-once-a-week.html.

Levinson, Kate. *Emotional Currency: A Woman's Guide to Building a Healthy Relationship with Money*. Berkeley, CA: Celestial Arts, 2011.

Long, Stephen D. *Divine Economy: Theology and the Market*. New York: Routledge, 2000.

Lui, Meizhu, Barbara Robles, Betsy Leondar-Wright, Rose Brewer, and Rebecca Adamson, with United for a Fair Economy. *The Color of Wealth: The Story Behind the U.S. Racial Wealth Divide*. New York, NY: The New Press, 2006.

Lutz, David W. "Christian Social Thought and Corporate Governance." In Kennedy, Athans, Brady, McDonough, and Naughton, eds., 121–140.

Marcuson, Margaret J. *Leaders who Last: Sustaining Yourself and Your Ministry*. New York: Seabury Books, 2009.

——————— *Money and Your Ministry*. Portland, OR: Marcuson Leadership Circle, 2014.

Matz, Brian. "The Principle of Detachment from Private Property in Basil of Caesarea's Homily 6 and Its Content." In Leemans, Matz, and Verstraeten, eds., 161–184.

McCarraher, Eugene. *The Enchantment of Mammon: How Capitalism Became the Religion of Modernity*. Cambridge, MA: The Belknap Press of Harvard University Press, 2019.

McKenna, Kevin E. *A Concise Guide to Catholic Social Teaching*, 3rd Ed. Notre Dame, ID: Ave Maria Press, 2019.

Murphy, James W, ed. *Faithful Investing: The Power of Decisive Action and Incremental Change*. New York: Church Publishing, 2019.

Murray, Julio E. "The AGAPE Economy: The Church's Call to Action." *The Anglican Theological Review*, 98, no. 1 (Winter 2016):122–136.

Notte, Jason. "Why Millennials Aren't Afraid to Talk about Money." TheStreet.com. November 8, 2017. https://www.thestreet.com/story/14355305/1/why-millennials-talk-about-money.html.

O'Brien Steinfels, Margaret. "The Contemporary Importance of Monsignor John A. Ryan and Catholic Social Thought." In Kennedy, Athans, Brady, McDonough, and Naughton, eds., 291–298.

Packer, Michael "Jesus Talked the Most About . . . Money?" Smyrna Patch. http://patch.com/georgia/smyrna/jesus-talked-the-most-aboutmoney.

Palmer, Parker. *Healing the Heart of Democracy: The Courage to Create A Politics Worthy of the Human Spirit*. San Francisco, CA: Jossey-Bass, 2011.

Patterson, Jane and Steven Tomlinson, "A Framework for Rule-Crafting Practice." Seminary of the Southwest, 2018.

Pawlikowski, John T. "Papal Teaching on Economic Justice: Change and Continuity." In Kennedy, Athans, Brady, McDonough, and Naughton, eds., 75–94.

Petrella, Ivan. *Beyond Liberation Theology: A Polemic*. London: SCM Press, 2008.

Poole, Eve. *Buying God: Consumerism & Theology*. London: SCM Press, 2018.

_____ *Capitalism's Toxic Assumptions: Redefining Next Generation Economics*. London: Bloomsbury, 2015.

Prentiss, Demi. *Making Money Holy*. New York: Church Publishing, 2020.

"Prosperity Gospel." Christianity Today. https://www.christianitytoday.com/ct/topics/p/prosperity-gospel/.

Radzins, Inese. "Althaus Reid Nov Notes," *Social Transformation and Liberation*. Pacific School of Religion, November 2017. https://moodle.gtu.edu/course/view.php?id=4289#section-13.

Rhee, Helen. "Wealth, Poverty and Eschatology." In Leemans, Matz, and Verstraeten, eds., 64–84.

Rieger, Jorge. *No Rising Tide: Theology, Economics and the Future.* Minneapolis, MN: Fortress Press, 2009.

Salvatierra, Alexia and Peter Heltzel. *Faith-Rooted Community Organizing: Mobilizing the Church in Service to the World.* Downers Grove, IL: IVP Books, 2014.

Schor, Juliet B. *Plentitude: The New Economics of True Wealth.* New York: Penguin Press, 2010.

Schut, Michael, ed. *Money & Faith: The Search for Enough.* New York: Morehouse Publishing, 2008.

Semega, Jessica, Melissa Kollar, Emily A. Shrider, and John Creamer, "Income and Poverty in the United States: 2019," U.S. Census Bureau, Report Number P60-270, September 15, 2020. https://www.census.gov/library/publications /2020/demo/p60-270.html.

Simonsen, Mario Henrique. *Brasil 2002,* 6th ed. Rio de Janiero: APEC, 1976.

Singh, Devin. *Divine Currency: The Theological Power of Money in the West.* Stanford, CA: Stanford University Press, 2018.

Skidelsky, Robert and Edward Skidelsky. *How Much is Enough? Money and the Good Life.* New York: Other Press, 2012.

Steinke, Peter L. *Congregational Leadership in Anxious Times.* Lanham, MD: Rowman & Littlefield, 2006.

_____ *Uproar: Calm Leadership in Anxious Times.* Lanham, MD: Rowman & Littlefield, 2019.

Sung, Jung Mo. *Desire, Market, and Religion.* London: SCM Press, 2007.

Tanner, Kathryn. *Christianity and the New Spirit of Capitalism.* New Haven, CT: Yale University Press, 2019.

_____ *Economy of Grace.* Minneapolis, MN: Fortress, Press, 2005.

_____ *Jesus, Humanity and the Trinity: A Brief Systematic Theology.* Minneapolis, MN: Fortress Press, 2001.

The Book of Common Prayer. New York, NY: Oxford University Press, 2007.

The Episcopal Church. "The Five Marks of Mission." http://www.episcopalchurch .org/page/five-marks-mission.

"The Most Dangerous Jobs for Men." CNBC. https://www.cnbc.com/2017 /01/04/the-10-most-dangerous-jobs-for-men.html.

The World Bank, "Poverty: Overview," October 7, 2020. https://www.worldbank .org/en/topic/poverty/overview.

Thornton, James. *Wealth and Poverty in the Teachings of the Church Fathers.* Manchester, MO: St. John Chrysostom Press, 1993.

United Nations, Millennium Goals. http://www.un.org/millenniumgoals/.

United Nations, Sustainable Development Goals. http://www.un.org/sustainable development/sustainable-development-goals.

Van Nuffelen, Peter. "Social Ethics and Moral Discourse in Late Antiquity." In Leemans, Matz, and Verstraeten, eds., 45–63.

Wallis, Jim. *Rediscovering Values: A Guide for Economic and Moral Recovery.* New York, NY: Howard Books, 2011.

Wariboko, Nimi. *God and Money: A Theology of Money in a Globalizing World.* Lanham, MD: Lexington Books, 2008.

Waters, Brent. *Just Capitalism: A Christian Ethic of Economic Globalization.* Louisville, KY: Westminster John Knox Press, 2016.

Welby, Justin. *Dethroning Mammon: Making Money Serve Grace.* London: Bloomsbury, 2016.

Wheeler, Sondra Ely. *Wealth as Peril and Obligation: The New Testament on Possession.* Grand Rapids, MI: Eerdmans, 1995.

Wilder, Barbara. *Money is Love: Reconnecting to the Sacred Origins of Money.* Santa Fe, NM: Wild Ox Press, 2010.

Williams, Rowan and Larry Elliott. *Crisis and Recovery, Ethics, Economics and Justice.* Houndmills, Basingstoke, Hampshire: Palgrave Macmillan, 2010.

Woodley, Randy S. *Shalom and the Community of Creation: An Indigenous Vision.* Grand Rapids, MI: William B. Eerdmans Publishing, 2012.

Zabriskie, Marek P., ed. *The Social Justice Bible Challenge: A 40 Day Bible Challenge.* Cincinnati, OH: Forward Movement, 2017.

CPSIA information can be obtained
at www.ICGtesting.com
Printed in the USA
JSHW050457180921
18825JS00005B/158

9 781640 654624